THE LAST
ORPHAN

THE LAST ORPHAN

When a journey of hope turns into a nightmare

REX WADE

MIRROR BOOKS

First published by Mirror Books in 2019

Mirror Books is part of Reach plc
10 Lower Thames Street
London EC3R 6EN
England

www.mirrorbooks.co.uk

ISBN 978-1-912624-32-4

FOR ANNIE, THE LOVE OF MY LIFE.

PROLOGUE.

ORANGES AND SUNSHINE

I'm high up on a grassy hill somewhere. I think it's over-looking the sea, but it might be inland – my memory isn't clear. It might be Polgooth, which isn't far from the fishing port of Mevagissey in south Cornwall, where I grew up with Margaret and James – and then, after James left, with Margaret and Pete. It's definitely somewhere in Cornwall, I know that much – but I cannot pinpoint exactly where it is. There's a caravan there, and a five-bar metal farm gate, with a woman leaning on it. That all seems quite normal, I suppose. But the frightening thing is that the woman has no face. No face at all. It's not that her face is turned away and I cannot see it – no, there's just a blank space where it ought to be.

This is the first thing I can remember, and it gives me chills every time I think about it. Is it a badly formed memory of my mum, I wonder? Or is it something deep in my brain trying to remember what her face looked like, but instead giving me a nightmarish vision of a woman I should know, who I have spent my whole life trying to find, but who has remained out of reach, inaccessible and unknowable?

Because the truth is that I never knew my mother – it took me decades to find out what happened to her after she left us. I grew up not even knowing whether she was alive or dead. I was probably three years old when I last saw her. She gave life to me and then, not long after that, she went away. My dad died soon after that, too. And then it was just me and my two brothers Kevin and Brucie, left to fend for ourselves in a big, bad world. We didn't – we couldn't – possibly know then, as defenceless little kids, just how big and just how bad it was. But we were about to find out.

*

Heligan Woods, South Cornwall, 1969

Kevin and I race through the woods, leaping over fallen trunks, our rucksacks clunking from side to side on our backs. Kevin, one year younger than me, is lighter and nimbler on his feet, and bombs ahead as we approach the clearing that leads towards Heligan Mill. He bustles through a tangle of low-lying branches, and races on ahead as they spring back into my face, whipping across my left cheek and momentarily blinding me. My howl of pain is met with a squeal of glee from up ahead, and I recover myself just in time to see him disappearing into a clump of trees at the edge of the woods.

As I take up the chase again, I catch glimpses of him darting through the undergrowth, ducking under branches and whooping triumphantly. I grit my teeth and run as fast as I can under the weight of my school bag. I round an enormous oak and as the mill looms into view, my little brother comes back into my line of sight. As he hurtles through the final stretch of woods, I see an enormous gnarled log on the path ahead of him. I close my eyes as I run and will him with all my might to trip over it. I can't let him beat me home. He leaps high into the air, and I swear out loud as he clears the branch with a final victorious shout. But his delight is short-lived, as he lands heavily on his right foot, stumbles and falls, his rucksack crashing down on the back of his head with a satisfying thud.

I roar like a wild animal as I catch up with my brother, jump over him and blast out into the open, passing the mill and tearing along the muddy track that leads to Rose Cottage. For those precious few moments as I blaze up the home straight, it feels as if a weight has been lifted from my shoulders. The wind rips through my hair and I don't have a care in the world. I raise my arms in celebration as I reach the end of the path, stagger up to the front of the house, and instantly double over to catch my breath.

Kevin, furious at his last-gasp blunder, tears up the path and sprints straight past me, crashing into the house through the rickety front door. I bolt in after him. Oblivious to the adults, we leap up the stairs and along the corridor to our bedroom and slam the door. We tear off our shoes, climb onto Bruce's bed and start jumping about on the springy mattress in a frenzy of energy and excitement. Bruce is way behind us – he thinks he's too grown up to join in our races these days – and if he knew we were bouncing on his bed, he'd kill us.

There are footsteps in the corridor. Kevin freezes. Sensing danger, I leap down from the bed and tiptoe across the room to my own, where I sit down and try to look as innocent as I can.

Pete slowly pushes open the door. We know it's him – since the day he arrived, we've been able to tell the difference between his heavy footsteps and Margaret's light steps on the creaky skirting boards – and anyway, Margaret always calls out our names before she reaches the door. We hold our breath, anxious not to make a sound or do anything that could make him angry. Whenever he decides we've done something to make him angry it doesn't end happily for us, and Margaret isn't strong enough to stop him.

Pete walks into the room and takes a long look at Kevin, then at me, and then stares at the two pairs of shoes lying at the foot of Bruce's bed. There is a long silence. Neither of us moves a muscle.

Pete looks at me again, and then at Kevin. Finally, he breaks the silence.

"You have a visitor."

Kevin and I gawp at each other. A visitor, for *us*?

Neither of us breathes a word.

"Well?" says Pete.

I swallow. "Who would want to visit us?"

His face darkens. I look down at my feet, anxious that I might have said something to upset him, but he doesn't reply.

"Who is it?" pipes up Kevin.

He puts his hands in his pockets. "Don't you want to come and find out?"

Kevin and I look at each other again in bewilderment. I open my mouth to speak, but nothing comes out.

"Fine," says Pete. "If you're not going to move your lazy arses, I'll send her up here."

He turns and walks out of the room.

Kevin is still looking at me. I know we're thinking the same thing: ever since we found out three years ago that Margaret isn't actually our mum, we've spent our lives wondering who our real parents are and when we'll meet them. Margaret has never told us anything about them, and I've spent three years feeling angry with her and confused about where my real mum went. And now there's a mysterious lady downstairs who wants to see us, but Pete won't say who she is.

We wait for what seems like hours for the lady to come up the stairs. My heart is racing. It's her. It's got to be. Who else would come specially to see us? Can it really be her?

The door opens a crack, and a stranger puts her head round the door.

"Hello, Rex. Hello, Kevin. Can I come in?"

My heart skips a beat and we stare at her, goggle-eyed.

"Okay," I gulp.

"Thank you," she whispers, as if we're all in on a big secret that Margaret and Pete know nothing about.

She smiles at us as she sits down carefully on Kevin's bed, folding her hands in her lap.

I can't keep it in any longer. "Are you our mum?" I blurt out.

Her eyebrows shoot up in surprise, and I instantly feel a wave of shame wash over me. Of course she's not our mum. Why did I let myself believe that she was? I'm an idiot. Kevin's face falls, too. How could we both be so stupid?

For a moment she seems to be at a loss for words, but then she relaxes, brushes her hair out of her face and clears her throat.

"No, Rex. I'm afraid I'm not."

"Who are you then?"

"My name's Dorothy, and I'm here to help you two. You're about to begin a new chapter in your lives, a very exciting one, and Margaret said that I could come and talk to you about what you want to do and where you'd like to go."

I'm beginning to feel uneasy by this point, and my palms are sweating. What is this "new chapter"? It sounds very mysterious, but why hasn't Margaret mentioned it before? Now that we know that she's not our real mum, does she not want us anymore?

"What do you mean, where we'd like to go?"

She smiles. "Well, now that Margaret's just had a baby, her life is going to be a lot more complicated, and it's going to be difficult for her to look after you as well. I'm from an organisation called Fairbridge, and we've come to help her find you a new home, one where you can be really happy. Even happier than you are here."

I wince. This woman knows that Margaret is kind and caring, but she doesn't have a clue about what Pete puts us through.

Neither Kevin nor I can find the courage to speak. We sit staring at her cautiously, wondering what she means by this "new home".

She smiles her mechanical smile once more. "I've talked to Margaret, and we've come up with three very exciting options for you. One possibility is that we could find you places at a boarding school—"

"What's a boarding school?" Kevin and I ask her in unison.

"It's a school where you live all year round, in a house with other boys. I'm sure you'd find it fun, wouldn't you?"

I think of the playground at school and imagine living in a house with Ant Miller. I shake the thought out of my head with a shudder.

"Or… if you don't like that idea… there's a lovely farm in another part of Cornwall where they're looking for two strong lads just like you. You could go and live there and help with the work after school each day."

I look at Kevin. That doesn't sound so bad. I like the outdoors, and I like animals.

"What's the third option?" Kevin asks.

"Well… the third option is the most exciting one of all." She looks around our bedroom, and her gaze comes to rest on the large map hanging on the wall above my bed. "Margaret tells me you've been doing a special project at school recently?"

I snap to attention. "We've been studying Australia." I point to it in the corner of the map. "There are lots of amazing animals that you never see here. Our teacher showed us pictures of them."

"It sounds like a wonderful place, doesn't it?" she says.

I pause and turn to look at her. I don't know what to say.

"And it's a wonderful place for children to grow up. The country of oranges and sunshine, that's what I call it. I know lots of people who've been there, and they all say it's beautiful. I think you'd be very happy living there. What do you think, Rex?"

"I don't know." It's true. I don't know. I like it here. I like Margaret. I don't like Pete, but Australia seems like a long way to go just to escape from him.

"I think it'd be the perfect place for you two. It would be different from your life here, but I think the change would be really good for you."

Something about this doesn't feel quite right. Has she forgotten?

"It's not just the two of us though," I remind her. "Bruce is coming too, isn't he?"

"Oh, of course," she replies without a moment's pause. "We never split up families."

She doesn't say much more, except to assure us how fantastic and exciting our life in Australia will be. Kevin and I listen in disbelief, unsure whether it's up to us or whether the decision has already been made for us, but we're thrilled all the same. Travelling to the other side of the world to start a new life – it all sounds so grand!

The lady smiles and smiles, and eventually she says goodbye and gets up to leave. It's all happened so quickly. Kevin and I share a bemused glance, before he lets out a whoop, and I leap off my bed and clamber back up onto Bruce's. We jump around to our hearts' content, not even caring whether Pete hears us.

PART I

CORNWALL

1.

WELCOME TO THE WORLD

Every morning, Bruce, Kevin and I run down to the stream with our buckets. As soon as we're out of the back door, the race is on. Down the hill, past the shed and out onto the muddy track. From there it's all about endurance – especially in winter, when the track is thick with mud and we have to jump to avoid the enormous icy puddles.

We run for what seems like miles, all the way down to the creek. We carry on along the bank for a little way, our buckets bumping against our legs, until we reach a small babbling spring, where we take it in turns to fill them up. Whoever arrives first gets to rest for a bit until the others have caught up, before we all turn and trudge back up the track with our heavy loads. It's a laborious journey, and we're lucky if we make it all the way home without slipping over in the mud and spilling the water on the way. If we do spill it, we have to go back down the hill to fill the bucket up again.

By the time we arrive back at Rose Cottage, we're freezing cold, hungry and our arms are exhausted. We always go out to the spring first thing in the morning – even if it's raining, hailing or snowing – otherwise we don't have any water to drink with our breakfast. But I like being outside at sunrise, so it doesn't seem like a chore. It gives us an opportunity for adventures. When we get to at the spring, I like to snack on the dewy sprigs of watercress that grow nearby. And sometimes the three of us cross the creek and head into the woods, where we climb the trees and pretend to be soldiers. If we've run there fast enough, we can spend a good few minutes playing. I run off to hide behind the trunks, before jumping out to ambush my brothers and shoot them down. Bruce and I chase Kevin back out of the woods, pelting him with imaginary bullets, over the creek. We race off back up the track only for Bruce to exclaim halfway up: "Oh God, we've forgotten the bloody buckets!"

We need the water from the spring for drinking, cooking, cleaning and washing. The taps in the house don't work and there's no electricity or gas. For hot water, we have to go out through the kitchen and the big lounge with the slate floor, and into the scullery where Margaret does all the laundry. There's a huge copper tub in there, which has a fire underneath it. That's where the water for the bath and for washing our clothes is heated. The bath – a big, galvanised thing – hangs on a hook outside, and every Sunday we bring it in and put it in front of the open fire in the lounge. Margaret fills it with hot water from the copper tub, and my brothers and I sit in the warm water in the flickering light of the fire and the paraffin lamp, while Margaret scrubs our backs. It's blissful during the frosty Cornish winters, and a blessed relief after freezing our toes off all week.

There's no toilet inside the house, so we have to go outside to a little privy, day or night. It's cold and dark at night-time, but there's paraffin lamp in the corridor and if I have to get up for a wee in the dark I always take a candle in a jar with me to light my way through the garden. We have to be careful about rats out in the toilet – once, I went outside with my candle to find a great big one sitting right on the toilet seat. I dropped the jam jar in terror and ran straight back into the house, without going to the toilet – I had to hold on until the sun rose the next morning, and I barely slept another wink!

But even with the rats, the cold, and the lack of water, Rose Cottage is still our paradise. Right in the middle of

Heligan Woods near Mevagissey, the gardens and trees are the best playground I can imagine. It is our magical universe – a dreamland where we feel completely removed from the rest of the world. The woods, which are full of knotted old oaks and elms, are wild and beautiful. In the autumn, I walk through them and there are huge piles of fallen leaves. I kick them, bury myself in them, and throw them over Kevin and Bruce. Sometimes I find a skeleton of a dead bird, which gives me a sad feeling in my stomach, and I pick it up and delicately carry it back to the house. Or I find skeleton leaves and carefully put them in my pocket. I take them home and keep them next to my bed. The natural world feels like a big blanket wrapped around us: it is safe and wonderful and I love it.

James and Margaret always tell us that we're wild and unruly boys. We spend hours after school making the most of the daylight, and come home covered in mud and with soaking wet clothes and scruffy hair, looking for more mischief. I don't know what James and Margaret do while we're at school, but I bet they don't have half as much fun as we do.

The wooden stairs in the narrow hallway are the best part of the house – we love stomping up and down them, making as much of a racket as we can. Margaret and James tell us off, but Margaret can never quite suppress a smile and I sometimes think she wants to join in with us. James and Margaret sleep in the bedroom on the left at the top of the stairs, and if you carry on down the corridor you get to the bedroom that I share with Kevin and Bruce. Bruce sleeps in the first bed that you come to as you open the door, on the left. Halfway along that wall is a window that looks out onto the woods, and Kevin and I have our beds on the far side of the room. Bruce is five years older than me – his bed is separate from me and Kevin, who are only a year apart. I suppose Kevin and I are closer to one another than either of us is to Bruce.

Bruce was born in 1955 and Kevin, who's the youngest, was born a year after me, in 1960. Margaret says we're all very different characters. She says I'm strong-willed and reckless, probably because I'm always dragging the others off on adventures. But I don't feel reckless – I actually feel quite shy inside and I like running off to explore the woods, because it's a place where the boys at school can't get at me. Being there makes me feel free. So when James calls me the difficult middle child I tell him that's unfair. Margaret says Kevin has more sense than me, but I think he likes our adventures just as much as I do. I'm not so sure about Bruce. He's bigger and stronger than we are, and he likes to remind us of both of these things, especially when he catches us bouncing on his bed.

The kitchen downstairs is old and beautiful, with an Aga, a big wooden table and a bench that is covered in marks and scratches. James splits logs on it, and we chip at it and scrape away at it during mealtimes, but it still looks beautiful because it is old and wooden and looks like it has always belonged there and will be there forever. The best thing about that kitchen, though, is the wonderful smells that come out of it when Margaret's cooking – there are always wonderful things appearing from the Aga, like homemade bread and seaweed jelly, which is one of my favourites.

Margaret says that Rose Cottage is a mile from our nearest neighbours. Every day on the way to school in Mevagissey we walk past Heligan Mill, where her friend Brenda lives – apart from that, our nearest neighbours are the people who live in Heligan House, which has lovely gardens. The narrow little track that leads up to Rose Cottage wends its way through an arch of rhododendrons, and as you emerge from the foliage you can see the cottage, surrounded by fields and trees – it's remote and quiet and beautiful. The cottage itself stands next to a stone bank, which provided the stone that was used to build it. It has a slate roof and on a good day I am able to leap from the bank onto the roof without injuring myself seriously, which has happened enough times. As you go in through the front entrance, there is a little porch with a huge set of cow horns above it. Those horns are another thing that I love about the place: they make it seem strange and mysterious and magical and exciting. On a bright, hot day, as you step under the horns into the porch and then onto the cottage's slate floor, the sudden cold on the soles of your feet and the darkness of the old stone house is refreshing and relaxing.

We call James and Margaret by their first names – we don't call them mum and dad. I don't know why, but we've done it for as long as I can remember so it doesn't seem strange to me, even though the boys at school tease me about it. They say that us Robsons aren't a real family and that nobody loves us. But we love our parents, Margaret especially, and know that she loves us, too. She lets us have fun at home, she is always there when we fall over and hurt ourselves, and she encourages us to work hard at school. She is also very clever – she studied Indian languages at Cambridge University, which is a very famous place all the way on the other side of the country. We want to be like her when we're older, because she is caring and affectionate and kind.

One day, I come back home from school to find Margaret sitting in the living room, wearing sunglasses. I stop at the top of the wooden stairs and look at her quizzically, my head cocked to one side. She smiles and takes her glasses off, revealing an enormous bee sting, right between her eyes – it is all swollen and red and it looks very painful. I say nothing, but just walk up to her and give her a hug. She hugs me back. I feel warm and safe.

2.

SURPRISES

"Hey, Golliwogs! Had a bath in the pig trough this morning?"

Pushing through the school gate, I glance up nervously to see Ant Miller and his mates swaggering towards me. Kevin has already run off into his classroom and Bruce is lagging behind – I'm on my own.

"You look like you've been dragged through a hedge backwards, Golliwog," shouts Tim Bale, Ant Miller's sidekick.

"Probably has been," another of his minions laughs. "Been drinking from puddles again, Golliwog?"

They call me Golliwog because of Robertson's jam. The labels have a picture of a black boy on them, and even though I've told them a million times that my name is Robson, not Robertson, they still haven't got the message.

"Been hugging trees again, flower boy?" Tim Bale sneers. Kevin and I are easy targets for them – they're all townies from Mevagissey, and we're the feral kids who live in the woods. Margaret and James aren't even from Cornwall, which doesn't help. We're not welcome here, and they like letting us know it at every opportunity.

My legs ache after the long walk from Rose Cottage. I try to run away before they can corner me, but it's too late. Ant Miller steps forward and backs me against the wall.

"You stink of cow shit, Golliwog," he hisses.

I stare at my feet. "My name's Robson," I mumble.

"Speak up, Golliwog! Talking to the flowers again? 'Ooh, my name's Rex Robertson and my best friend's a dandelion'," he chants.

"My name's Robson, not Robertson, I say. "Idiot."

That wipes the smile off his face. "What did you call me?"

"Idiot. You're a stupid idiot. You don't even know my—"

A series of colours flash through my vision and I feel a sudden aching pain in the side of my head. Ant Miller aims a second punch at my stomach and I double up against the wall. He steps back to aim a vicious kick at me, but I launch myself off the wall with all my might, headbutting him in the midriff and knocking him to the ground. My head is spinning and my vision is blurry. I don't know what to do next.

For some reason, Ant Miller's mates have all scattered. He doesn't get up, but lies on the ground beneath me, moaning theatrically. That's when I look up to see our teacher Mr Maloney standing five metres away, his stern gaze locked on me.

"Robson. Follow me. Now!"

There's no use arguing with him. It always seems to be me who gets caught when I'm only fighting back. Still feeling dizzy, I follow him to the classroom, where he gives me four smart whacks with the slipper. I don't care much about getting the slipper – it's nothing compared to the pain I'm already in – but seeing Ant Miller get away scot-free makes me boil inside. By the time the teacher has opened the door and ordered me back out into the playground, he's got up and is joking around with his followers again.

One of the teases I hate most is when they mock me for not having a television. We've never had one – I hardly even know what they look like. For all the positives of living in the middle of the woods, our life at Rose Cottage sometimes feels insular and isolated, and not having a TV or electricity or running water like everyone else can make it hard to make friends. I was born seven years ago, on 9 January 1959, which a teacher at school says was just a few days after the Soviet Union sent the first satellite into space. But that sort of thing seems very far away from our lives – travelling into space is almost unimaginable when you have to walk for miles just to get to school.

But our long walk each day gives us some good opportunities to get revenge on the bullies. Kevin and I often arrive late for school because we get distracted on the way. To get there we have to walk through the woods into a caravan site, and then down a gravel track. We cross the main road, walk along a concrete side road, up a flight of stone steps and down another track, and we're there. Along the way we pass a lot of fields where cows sometimes graze. Whenever we see them, we grin at each other, take out the combs we carry in our back pockets and jump over a stile into the field. We giggle with delight as we run our combs through the nearest cowpat, before leaping back over the stile and running the rest of the way to school, holding the stinky combs at arm's length. At school, we hide the combs behind our backs so that no one can see them, before sneaking up on Tim Bale or another one of Ant's cronies and wiping the combs through his hair. Their squeals of disgust send us into hysterics, and we run off to the other side of the playground as fast as we can.

The natural world has always fascinated me. I love talking to the wildlife around where we live and writing about the countryside. I especially like writing poetry and drawing pictures. At school, the other kids sometimes find my drawings and poems and start passing them round class and laughing at them. They call me a sissy and beat me up in the playground, but I find nature and wildlife more beautiful than anything in the world and I won't let anyone stop me enjoying them. Whenever Kevin and I run into the fields to put our combs in the cowpats, I always let him go first and pause for a second to go up to the cows. I hold my hand out flat and then stroke them gently on the face or between the ears. They look at me serenely and gently lean into my palm. Their skin is coarse and warm to the touch and they breathe heavily through their huge nostrils. At home, I like to sit in the rhododendrons at the front of the house, waiting for a bee to land on the flowers. When it settles and dips into a flower to get the nectar, I reach out a finger and gently stroke the back of it.

One day when we come home from school, Margaret is waiting at the front of the house with a curious little smile on her lips. As we say hello, she looks at me and holds out her hand. I take it and look up at her.

"I have a surprise for you," she grins.

"What is it?"

She says nothing in reply, but leads me around to the back of the house. Next to the privy, the shed door is standing wide open, and through it I see a gorgeous goat. I can scarcely contain myself.

"A goat! Is it a he or a she?"

"It's a she – a nanny goat. Do you like her?"

"I love her!" I approach the goat cautiously and hold out my hand. She eyes me with suspicion and then takes a small tentative step forward and nudges her nose against my hand. She smells a bit funny, but seems friendly.

"What shall we call her?" asks Margaret.

My eyes light up. "Nanny!"

Milking the goat soon becomes part of Margaret's daily routine, and she uses the milk to make delicious cottage cheese, which we eat on freshly baked bread after school. Nanny makes me love and respect animals even more. She is so calm and gentle, and never hurts me for no reason like the teachers or the boys at school do. She's easy to understand and likes being looked after. Nothing is complicated with her.

I want to have more pets when I'm older – animals show me more love than anyone. Apart from Margaret and my brothers, that is. Since we got Nanny, I've been looking out for wild animals even more. My heart misses a beat with excitement on our morning trips to the spring whenever I catch sight of an owl in the woods, or a bat or a deer staring out at me from between the trees.

*

"Boys, can you come to the kitchen, please."

"Why?"

"Please, just come down. It's important." Margaret looks pale and her hands are clasped nervously over her stomach. I want to run over and give her a hug, but she's avoiding my gaze, so I think better of it. She turns around and walks through the living room and down the creaky stairs.

Bruce, lying on his bed, rolls his eyes and gets up sluggishly. Kevin and I obediently follow suit and go downstairs in silence.

Margaret is sitting at the kitchen table, scratching its wooden surface with a fingernail. There are red rings round her eyes and the skin above her top lip looks red, as if she has been crying. I've never seen her cry before.

The silence seems to last forever as we shuffle along the bench to make room for each other. When we're all sat down, Margaret sniffs and clears her throat, before looking up at us, wide-eyed, like a lost animal.

"Boys, I've got some news. I think it's best to tell you right away, as you'd find out soon enough anyway. James has decided not to live with us anymore. He's moving away. It's just going to be me and you three from now on."

Kevin and I exchange glances. Bruce looks at Margaret, motionless. None of us knows what to say.

"Why doesn't he want to live with us anymore?" Kevin's voice has been reduced to a whisper.

Margaret swallows. "He doesn't—" She chokes on her words. "He says he doesn't love me anymore and that he thinks it's best if he goes and lives somewhere else. I know it will be hard for you to lose him, but I promise you that nothing else will change. I love the three of you and we will make the best of this and have a good time on our own, won't we?"

I smile weakly. I feel sorry for Margaret and hate seeing her so hopeless like this, but I know that as long as we still have our mum, we will manage.

I know a boy at school whose dad went away, and his family ended up using a different name. "Will we have to change our surname?" I ask.

Margaret hesitates. She seems lost for words. "Well... Robson isn't actually your real name, is it, so eventually that'll be up to you, Rex."

Kevin and I look at each other incredulously. Not our real name? We both look at Bruce, but he doesn't flinch – this news doesn't seem to have taken him by surprise at all. I open my mouth and then shut it again, like a goldfish, confused. "If that's not my real name, why did you tell us it is?"

At school I'm called Rex Robson, and Margaret calls me Rex Robson if I've done something naughty and she's telling me off. Have my parents and my teachers been lying to me all this time? Why would they do something like that?

"Well, Rex, you remember when I first met you a few years ago at the home in Newquay?"

Kevin and I look at each other again. Then we both look blankly at Margaret.

"You remember, when James and I came to pick you up and brought you here for the first time?"

My stomach suddenly feels empty, and I realise that I have no memory of anything before Rose Cottage – it's all I've ever known. Rex Robson is the only name I know, and Margaret and James are the only parents I know. I've never even thought of questioning this – why should I? But now, all of a sudden, I have a thousand questions about how I got here and whether Margaret and James have really known me since the very beginning.

"Don't you remember it at all, boys?"

Bruce is staring at the table now, but has not moved an inch. Kevin and I are squirming in our seats, struggling to remember what we're being asked and overwhelmed by the enormity of Margaret's questions. Suddenly I can feel a big hole opening up in my life, a void in my memory that I never knew existed.

"Rex, Kevin, Bruce... You can each decide on the name you want to choose because your real surname isn't Robson. And James and I aren't your actual parents."

Kevin's eyes are out on stalks.

"Boys, your real parents were from another part of Cornwall. Your father died when you were very little and your mum couldn't manage, so they gave you to us to look after instead. I'm so sorry. I thought you would have remembered some of this."

I feel like something inside me has gone missing, and I suddenly feel uneasy sitting at the table, next to my brothers, with a woman who I always thought was my mum. If Margaret isn't really our mum, does she love us? I can't believe that anymore. And if she could lie to us like that, how can I trust anything she's said? The person I thought loved me more than anyone else in the world has betrayed me.

And then some more pressing questions come into my head. If Margaret and James aren't my real parents, who are? And why did they not want me?

Bruce still hasn't said a word. I wonder whether he knows some of this already – he's much older than me, so perhaps he remembers. Surely he'd have known that our dad was dead? But I don't want to ask him about any of this in front of Margaret. I decide to ask him tomorrow morning, when we go down to the spring.

But when I get up the next day, there's no sign of Bruce anywhere. He's left his bed unmade, his belongings are scattered around his end of the room, and he is nowhere to be found.

Margaret is worried. "I've no idea where he could have gone. This is the last thing any of us need right now," she quivers.

Kevin and I trudge down to the spring to fetch the water in silence. We don't go into the woods to play soldiers today, and on the way back up the hill the buckets of water feel heavier than usual.

When Kevin and I come back from school, Margaret is in a state.

"Was Bruce there at school today?"

We shake our heads. He didn't turn up at school and there's still no sign of him at home. I don't want to talk to Margaret much, but I have some burning questions after yesterday's conversation that I need to get off my mind. I turn to face her.

"If Robson isn't our actual name, what is it?"

Margaret sighs. "Wilton, Rex. Your dad's surname was Wilton."

"Like the carpets?"

"Yes Rex, like Wilton Carpets."

I pause to think about this for a moment, before raising my head and looking her dead in the eye. "I'm Rex Wilton, then. That's my name from now on." I turn my back on her and stomp up the stairs and down the corridor to my room, with Kevin hurrying along behind me.

A few days later, Bruce is back, but he won't tell us where he's been. Margaret asks him again and again what he was thinking, where he went, and why he didn't tell anyone. She asks whether he has a girlfriend he went to see, but I don't believe he would run away without telling anyone just because of a girl. Kevin and I don't ask him any more questions – we try to go back to our daily routine of fun and games, of running down to the spring every morning and racing each other back from school. But something doesn't feel quite right. Some of the magic of Rose Cottage has gone.

I decide to stick with my decision and keep my dad's name, Wilton. If it was the name I was born with, it's what I want to be called now. But from that day on, I start to get into trouble more often. Something in me feels bolder and more fearless. I don't want to try and do well at school to please Margaret anymore. I don't want to be bullied. I want to stand up for myself and fight back against the people that have hurt me. But at the same time I somehow feel smaller inside, like I don't know how to fill the gap that my old name has left. And I begin to rebel in small ways that gradually get worse and worse. Especially when Pete arrives on the scene.

3.

Paradise Lost

About three hundred yards from where we live, there's a little clearing in the woods. Every autumn, Kevin and I gather all the leaves from around the edge of the clearing and heap them up into an enormous pile in the middle, before taking it in turns to dive headfirst into it. Or we climb the trees around the clearing and make wild animal noises to each other across the open space. If Kevin doesn't want to come outside, I like to go there anyway and sit at the top of a tree, all alone. I stay absolutely silent, not moving a muscle, and hope that a deer or hare might pass through.

Several months have passed since our conversation with Margaret and we're doing our best to forget about it, but we can never quite manage that completely. We don't want to talk about it anymore, either to each other or to Margaret. It makes me sad to think about her not being my real mum, and when it does cross my mind I stop wanting to play games or go outdoors.

Margaret gets us some guinea pigs to keep in the shed. They have soft fur and nuzzle against my fingers when I stroke their faces. I love to pick them up and feel them breathing as I hold them in my arms. It feels like they trust me, and I can trust them too.

Bruce doesn't reply if we ever try to ask him about why he disappeared. He seems more distant from us now, but I think Kevin and I are closer since Margaret told us about our mum and dad. We feel the same things and try to cheer each other up when we're sad.

One day after school Margaret tells Kevin and me to go and play outside, and we bomb out of the door, pretending to be Spitfires. Weaving through the trees towards the clearing, I see a sudden movement and a flash of colour. I stop dead in my tracks and listen. Kevin catches up with me and peers inquisitively through the trees. We can hear a sort of flapping noise, how I imagine an enormous exotic bird might sound as it takes flight. But then we hear a grunt and a voice muttering something in a strange accent that I don't recognise. Kevin stifles a giggle, and I put a finger to my lips.

We tiptoe forwards as quietly as we can, wincing at the sound of the twigs crunching and splintering beneath our feet. Once we are within a few metres of the clearing, we can see the cause of the noise: a short bald man with a beard is struggling to put up a bright red tent, which is flapping violently in the wind. His face is scrunched up in concentration and he is oblivious to our presence, cursing aloud as he struggles to jam a peg into the ground.

I take the lead, sidling up to the nearest tree and waiting for the man to go to the far side of his tent before climbing up into the branches. I reach down to give Kevin a hand up and we crouch among the leaves, peering down at the stranger like a pair of curious monkeys. He's at the other end of the tent now, grabbing at the loose fabric that's flapping above his head and trying to pin it down. He's too short to get hold of it properly, though, and the sight of him jumping up and down and violently swearing is too much for us to bear. Kevin splutters in a desperate attempt to suppress a laugh, and suddenly I can't hold it in anymore either.

He turns sharply and looks around, his face like thunder. Eventually he spots us and strides over.

"What are yous laughing about then? Gonna help us or what?"

Kevin and I look at each other and burst out laughing – his accent is like nothing we've ever heard. For a moment he looks like he's going to explode, but then his face softens and his lip curls into something resembling a smile.

"Aye, alright then. Suit yourselves."

He seems amused at the sight of us hopping around in the trees, and I wriggle along a branch extending over the clearing to get a closer look at him.

"Where are you from, mister?"

"Edinburgh, pal. Came all the way down from Scotland and I can't even get me bloody tent up."

"So what are you doing here?"

"What does it look like I'm doing?"

"Can we help you with it?" Kevin chimes in.

"No, son, you're alright."

We ask him some more questions, enthralled by his funny accent and his bald head. He plays along and asks us where our mum is.

"She's not here. We're on our own," I say, puffing out my chest.

"You boys from round here then?" he asks.

"Just over there," Kevin pipes up, pointing in the direction of the cottage.

"Is that right? You got other brothers and sisters?"

"Yeah, a big brother called Bruce," I say. "What's your name?"

"What's yours?" he replies. And after a moment's pause, he adds, "I'm Pete."

"I'm Rex and this is Kevin," I say from my perch in the tree. "Our mum's called—" I catch myself in the act – I called her our mum – and feel ashamed, but I don't know what else to call her. "She's called Margaret."

"Aye? And what's your dad's name?"

Kevin and I exchange a quick glance.

"We haven't got a dad."

I don't want to tell him any more, so leap down out of the tree and scramble off into the forest with Kevin in hot pursuit, peppering me with squealing bullets from his imaginary machine gun.

A week or so later we're lugging our buckets of water up the track towards the cottage when we catch sight of Pete coming down the hill towards us. He puts a hand to his forehead to shield his eyes from the sun, and when he realises that it's us, a smirk spreads across his face.

"You lads are out and about nice and early. Want a hand with them buckets?"

We grunt our appreciation and he takes them from us, before turning round and walking up the track with us towards the cottage.

"That your house up at the top, then?"

I nod.

"Nice place. Where's your big brother?"

"He didn't want to come with us," says Kevin. "He said we didn't need an extra bucket, now that James isn't here anymore."

"Who's James, then? Your dad?"

We look at our feet and don't reply.

"Aye, I see." He stares in the direction of the house.

The rest of the journey passes in silence and when we arrive, Pete comes into the kitchen with us to put the buckets down. When Margaret comes through from the living room she stops in her tracks, taken aback by the sight of the squat stranger standing between us.

"Boys, who's this? You haven't made him carry your buckets all the way up the hill, have you?"

"His name's Pete and he's from Edinburgh," Kevin says. "He said he wanted to help us with the buckets."

Pete chuckles and holds out a hand to Margaret. "Pete Smith. I'm staying nearby. Bumped into these lads on the way and they looked like they needed a hand, so—"

"We didn't *need* help!" I interject angrily.

"Now, now, Rex, that's enough," says Margaret, taking his hand. "Well, thank you, Mr Smith, that's very kind of you. Would you like to stay for a cup of tea now that you're here? I'm afraid it'll take a little while, but—"

"That'd be lovely," Pete butts in, looking at her with a curious smile. "Thanks very much, —"

"—Margaret," she replies hurriedly.

"Thank you, Margaret."

Kevin and I have no idea why Pete is camping out in the woods in Mevagissey, but when we come home from school in the afternoon he's still sitting at the kitchen table with Margaret, and it looks like they haven't moved all day. Margaret looks happier than she has in weeks, and she briskly turns to say a quick hello to us without seeming to notice the bruise on my forehead from the playground today, before resuming her conversation with Pete.

Pete glances round. "Hello, lads," he says in a voice that seems softer than before, turning back to Margaret before we can reply. We run straight up to our room, and Bruce casts them a dark look as he walks through the kitchen.

The next morning we trudge back up the hill with our water to find Pete waiting for us a little higher up the track than the previous day. He reaches out for the buckets and we hand them to him without a word. Margaret offers him breakfast when we arrive, and he's still there, leaning against the kitchen wall, when we come back from school.

Before long, he stops helping us carry the water home, but by the time we arrive for breakfast with the buckets he's already in the kitchen, waiting for his cup of tea. When we ask Bruce about it, he mumbles that Pete treats us like a hotel and says something nasty about Margaret that upsets me.

Things move quickly and within weeks, Pete takes his tent down and moves into our house. He makes himself at home very quickly: the day after he moves in, I come home to find him sitting on the living room floor with his legs crossed, his eyes closed, and his fingers and thumbs pressed together, making a strange humming sound.

"What are you doing, Pete?"

He stops humming and opens his eyes, looking at me as if I've just trodden on his foot.

"I'm meditatin', son," he says sternly. "Can't you see? I need a bit of peace and quiet right now, so run along."

I have no idea what "meditating" means, and him sitting in my house and telling me what to do makes me cross. I stomp up to my room, dump my bag, and run outside to get away from him.

*

"Where's my newspaper, son?"

"I forgot it."

"Why did you forget it?"

"I don't know."

"I need it now, son. No breakfast without a newspaper. You'd better nip out and get it for me, sharpish."

I grit my teeth and head back out to the village. When I bring him his newspaper, he angrily tells me that I've bought the wrong one, calls me stupid, and asks why I haven't filled up the copper tub with water this morning. I tell him it was because I was out buying his newspaper, and that he can do it himself. He's a grown man and could easily carry two buckets back from the spring when we're lucky to make it up the hill with one – why should we do everything for him? He snorts and calls me a lazy sod.

*

"Pete's going to help us mend the shed, aren't you, Pete? Isn't that great, boys?"

Pete is standing smugly next to Margaret outside our bedroom, blocking the doorway as if the whole house belongs to him.

"We don't need his help – we can do it ourselves," I snort. The guinea pigs in the shed are mine, and it should be my job to make sure they're warm and protected, especially with winter fast approaching.

"Now, I'm not sure that'd be such a good idea, would it, son?" says Pete.

"I'm not your son."

Pete's face flushes scarlet and he flashes me a fierce look, pointing at each of us in turn. "Don't you go doing anything silly now, boys. The walls are coming off that shed and it needs a proper repair job. You need experience for that sort of thing. It's not for you to touch."

Margaret seems uneasy and tries to usher Pete out of the room, but he lingers in the doorway for a moment longer and holds my gaze, his dark eyes glinting in the light from the paraffin lamps. My insides are boiling with anger and my stomach is fluttering.

Margaret and Pete retreat to the living room and I turn to Kevin and say, "We're fixing that shed, whether he likes it or not."

"Yeah!" whispers Kevin.

The following day is a Saturday and Pete goes into the village for the afternoon. Kevin and I dash into the shed and look for a hammer and some nails. The top of the wall that's furthest from the house is coming loose, leaving big gaping holes in the corners. Kevin passes me the nails and I stand on tiptoes to hammer them through the splintered wood, nailing the wall securely to where it joins the roof – I'm just tall enough to reach. Then I hop over to fix the other end and hammer in a row of nails along the top of the wall to make sure it stays in place. We use all the nails we can find and when I step back to admire my work, the wall looks firm and secure. It might not be the tidiest job in history, but the holes are fixed and now the guinea pigs won't get cold or rained on. I'm pleased with our work and we put the hammer back and run off into the woods to play soldiers.

When we come down for breakfast the next day, Pete is waiting for us at the table. He gets up from the bench as soon as we step through the door and silently beckons us outside.

Kevin and I follow him sheepishly. We know what this is going to be about, but there's nothing we can do. He heads around the back of the shed and we trail after him, dragging our feet. Standing with his hands on his hips, he looks at the wall of the shed, his head cocked to one side.

"So, boys. Either of you know anything about this?"

Kevin looks at me. I stand as tall as I can and look Pete squarely in the face.

"I know about it. We fixed the shed, because it's ours and it was broken."

"*Your* shed? Is that right?" A thundercloud passes over his face.

"Yes. It's ours, so we mended it."

Then Pete grabs me by my shirt and slams my back into the rickety wall with unbelievable force. My head spins and I struggle for breath beneath his hairy arm that's pinning my chest against the wall.

"*You* mended it? You remember I told you not to?"

I splutter in reply, unable to speak.

"Remember? Or are you really that stupid?"

I nod my head weakly.

He lets me go and drags us both inside the shed, where he points at the rows of nails protruding through the wall. "And you really think that's a good idea? Nails stickin' out in every direction in our bloody shed? Are you stupid?" His voice becomes hoarse and incomprehensible as he rants and raves.

Kevin and I are stunned into silence, but he clouts me around the head with the palm of his hand. "Answer me!" he bellows.

"It's not your shed," I hiss through gritted teeth. "This is our house."

The next few seconds are a haze. I see Pete bending over to pick up a plank of wood lying on the floor of the shed, and the next thing I know I'm lying with my cheek on the grubby wooden floor and a splitting pain in the side of my throbbing head. Kevin unsteadily raises himself to a sitting position, nursing his side.

For all his sleepy humming on the living room floor, Pete is not a peaceful man, and as the months go by, he begins to treat us even worse. Early one Sunday morning I go out to milk Nanny, avoiding Pete, who I heard having an argument with Margaret in their bedroom before breakfast. When I get to the shed, I realise that I've forgotten to bring the saucepan that I put the milk in, so I dash back inside and run straight into Pete, stepping on his foot as my head collides with his ribs.

"What are you playing at, you little shit?" he barks, shoving me off him.

"I… just need a saucepan for Nanny."

"A saucepan, eh? Let me get that for you," he growls.

He paces through the kitchen and swaggers back, the pan in his right hand.

"Next time, you look where you're going, son."

The saucepan flies towards me and catches me on the side of my head. I fall to the floor as he yells something at me that I can't understand. Hearing my screams, Margaret flies into the room. She grabs Pete's arms to restrain him, but he wheels round and shoves her away, before dropping the pan, grabbing hold of her by the hair, and throwing her to the floor. As Margaret and I lie sobbing in a heap on the floor, Pete turns and stomps upstairs, slamming the bedroom door behind him.

*

We knew we weren't a real family before Pete arrived, but Margaret is the closest thing I've got to a mother and Rose Cottage the closest thing I've ever had to a home. Life in Heligan Woods makes me feel really happy inside and there are things about being there that I still love, but having Pete at home is like living with Ant Miller, except Pete is bigger and stronger and I make him angry even when I try not to. There isn't enough room for all five of us in the house, and it feels like Pete has begun to tear our little family unit apart.

One afternoon, Bruce comes home and Pete is standing in the corridor, blocking the way and wanting to know where he's been. Bruce refuses to tell him, so Pete shoves him and throws all sorts of filthy insults at him. Suddenly, Bruce launches himself at Pete and grabs hold of his beard, tearing a handful of it right out. Pete roars in pain and flies at Bruce, showering him with punches to the head and stomach, while Bruce tries to fight back. Margaret intervenes and sends the three of us to our room, while trying to calm Pete down. When we get upstairs, I tell Bruce he's an idiot for attacking Pete, but he flies off the handle and punches me in the face. I'm angry and confused so I hit Kevin, and in the ensuing racket Pete storms in to our room and gives us all a thrashing.

The next morning Bruce is gone, but Pete doesn't care – if anything, it seems to lift a weight off his shoulders and he struts around the house even more confidently.

Pete seems to like Margaret, but I don't think he likes children. He just wants us out of his way – maybe he knows that Margaret isn't our real mum.

*

One night, I wake up busting for a wee. I grope around on my bedside table for the jar I keep with a candle in it, but suddenly I freeze. There are raised voices coming from the other end of the corridor, a rapid, high-pitched, stammering babble and the menacing rumble of a man's voice. Suddenly there's a scream. I jump to my feet, unsure of what to do. Another piercing scream sends a shudder through my whole body. I creep out into the corridor. I don't dare light the candle. The door to Pete and Margaret's room is shut, and the voices from within are even more agitated. Pete's voice rises over Margaret's and I feel a thud that shakes the wooden floor I'm standing on. The voices stop and all I can hear is quiet sobbing. Then Pete mutters something, and her crying becomes more violent.

I stand stock still for a whole minute, listening for Margaret's voice, but there are no more words and no more screams. I edge down the corridor towards the toilet but stop in my tracks. My pyjamas are wet around my thighs and I don't need to go anymore.

4.

AND THEN THERE WERE SIX

Bruce comes back. With four males all vying for domination, the house begins to feel like a warzone. All Bruce, Kevin and I want is to stay with Margaret, but we are afraid that we're losing her to Pete and we don't understand why. Pete beats us and he beats Margaret. We can't work out why she doesn't throw him out, but when we ask her why she likes him, her response is always the same: "He's got a kind heart and he makes me laugh. He might not always show it, but I think he really cares about us all."

And it's true that he isn't always a complete bastard. One Saturday afternoon in the spring, he comes home with a vinyl album tucked under his arm and a huge grin on his face.

This baffles me. "Pete, why have you got a vinyl record when we don't have a record player?" We don't even have electricity, so the record wouldn't be much good even if we did have a player.

He raises his eyebrows and chuckles. "We'll see, pal. I'll find a way."

Perhaps he's going to take it to someone else's house to play it there, but whatever his plan is, he doesn't get the chance to listen to it. He leaves it lying on a chair in the living room and the next day, when Kevin and I are in there chatting to Margaret, he walks in and sits down absentmindedly. There's a sound of cracking vinyl from underneath him.

Kevin and I go rigid, fearing one of his explosions. But instead, he looks up and stares at us with an expression of comic surprise, and says, "It sounds like a broken record!" He laughs, and so do we, but we all know that if we had broken his record it would be a different story.

Each summer, Margaret's parents Alex and Ida rent a cottage in Mevagissey for a few weeks. When they arrive, they always come to Rose Cottage with a gift for me and my brothers: an envelope stuffed with threepenny bits, which usually amounts to about £5. We're always overjoyed, and they take us into town to spend it. They also go on long walks in the woods with us, and they laugh at the games we play. They must be in their sixties, but they still join in with us and we love spending time with them. These summers are wonderful and remind us what being part of a family is all about.

But when Alex and Ida go home to Kent, Pete's bullying picks up where it left off. Added to that, Ant Miller is picking on me more than before – the cuts and bruises I get at school are worse than ever, and still the teachers still seem to blame me every time. But I refuse to accept it and start to rebel, fighting back in the only way I've come to know. One day, when one of Ant Miller's mates calls me Golliwog, I launch myself at him with my fists like Pete would, kicking out viciously and shouting obscene insults and tearing at his hair. And the more fights I get into with the bullies, the more I start to take out my anger on the kids who are younger and smaller than me.

The more trouble I get into at school, the more distant Margaret is with me. The first time my teacher tells her that I've been beating up kids for their pocket money, she's upset and tries to reason with me.

"Rex, how could you? Never, ever hit people, it's a horrible thing to do. Those boys did nothing to hurt you, so why are you hurting them?"

But I just stand there in silence and stare at her. She doesn't stop Pete from hitting us at home, so it seems unfair of her to be angry at me for doing the same thing.

But the teachers keep on calling her in to school to talk about my behaviour and she looks more exhausted every time she has to tell me off. And more and more, I feel as if she doesn't understand me, as if I don't know her anymore, as if I'm a burden on her. As if we all are, apart from Pete – and yet we were happier all together before he arrived.

Little by little, I begin to do other naughty things. One day, Pete hits me for no reason, so I run away. I just go. I want to get away from the house, and from the angry voices, the fists, the blaming. I run through the fields into Mevagissey, past the church and into the graveyard, and I slam the gate behind me. I sit on the ground and pluck at the grass, tearing the stems apart in my hands. The late summer evening is warm and pleasant. It's quiet here and I don't want to go home – I want to stay here all day, all year, forever.

But by dinnertime, I'm hungry. I don't want to go home, but I don't have any money to buy food, so I get up and walk around the graveyard, looking for an apple tree or a blackberry bush. But there is no food to be found, only flowers of all colours adorning the graves. Eventually I give up – my stomach gets the better of me and I turn to go home. But then I have a flash of inspiration. I look at the flowers, which are crisp and fresh and look like they've come straight from a market stall. So, without thinking and led entirely by my hunger and my fear of home, I grab a bunch of flowers from the nearest grave, dash out of the gate and cross the road to the row of houses opposite the church. I knock on a front door and a hunched old lady opens it, peering out into the evening light.

"Hello," I say, looking as innocent as I can. "Would you like to buy some flowers?"

"Oh, thank you, dear, how lovely! Look at those, aren't they beautiful. Now, let's see, you just wait there a minute, and I'll go and get my purse."

And so I start going from door to door in the village, selling flowers. And when I've sold all the flowers from the first bunch, I go back to the graveyard for more. It's a fun prank to play, I can buy bread with the money, and it helps me to forget the cuts and bruises I've been struggling to ignore.

I begin to make more and more frequent trips to the graveyard, until a few weeks later a middle-aged woman opens the door.

"Yes?" she says brusquely.

"Would you like to buy some flowers?"

She looks down at the pot I'm holding and eyes me suspiciously.

"Where did you get that pot?"

"I… er…" Stupidly, I haven't thought of a cover story.

"Well?"

I don't know what to say. Suddenly, my stomach is churning and my legs are shaking with nerves.

"You got them from the graveyard, didn't you? You know whose grave you took those from?"

I don't know where to look and shake my head guiltily.

"You horrible boy! Stealing from my own mother's grave and selling the flowers back to me? How dare you!"

She grabs me by the ear and drags me back to the graveyard. She makes me put the flowers back, and marches me home.

Margaret is devastated when she finds out that I've been stealing. She doesn't forgive me for days, but I don't care – I feel like she and Pete are the reason for all this and that I wouldn't be getting into trouble if it wasn't for them.

But eventually, I realise that my biggest fear is becoming a reality: we are losing the one person in our lives who has always given us real love and comfort. Margaret spends more and more time with Pete now, and less and less with us. And though Pete isn't always bad, his temper flares almost every day. He's always trying to find fault with us, and we have no escape. When he says we've done something wrong, Margaret believes him, and she never seems to stand up for us.

And so we find ways to take our revenge. In the winter of 1968 there's heavy snow, which is a rare event so close to the coast, and we decide to make the most of it. The three of us heave the bathtub down from its hook and drag it up to the meadows, along with the peg that we use to stake Nanny's leash in the ground. We lug the bathtub all the way to the top of a hill and then the three of us jump in and career down the hill, using it as an enormous sledge. The bathtub hurtles down, out of control, and we roar with delight. I'm manning the brakes: as we get to the bottom of the slope I ram the peg through the plughole and into the ground, in an attempt to regain control. But it doesn't stop us in time – the bath speeds along and smashes into a large tree stump, which crushes the front of the bath completely.

When he sees the three of us scampering back towards the house, dragging the caved-in tub behind us, Pete loses his rag. He comes outside and gives each of us a good clout, but we don't care one bit – we've really stuck it to him. None of us are able to have a bath until months later, when Margaret and Pete can afford a new one. In the meantime we have to stand in front of the basin and wash ourselves with cloths. Pete really takes it out on Bruce and accuses him of being the ringleader of the bath prank.

And eventually Bruce can't take Pete's bullying anymore. He begins to run off more and more frequently, and it gets to the point when he has fallen out with Pete so badly that that he is no longer living with us most of the time. We later discover from Margaret that he has gone to stay with Alex and Ida in West Wickham in Kent.

In the spring of 1969, there is some big news – Margaret is pregnant. Kevin and I feel like she's had enough of us and wants her own children. I tell him that we knew she wasn't really our mum all along and so we should have expected this.

Soon our troublemaking is in full swing. Kevin is mischievous, but I'm much worse. I begin to dupe him into helping me with my thieving. In the bluebell season, I tell him about an adventure I'm going on to the graveyard, and that we will be able to make a few bob along the way. We take the flowers and put bags of them into fertiliser sacks, before selling them door to door. The number of people who buy them for a shilling a bunch is amazing, and we make several pounds each time we do it.

Mevagissey is a lovely place – I suppose it's what you might call a traditional Cornish fishing village, so there are always a lot of tourists there in the summer. They're easy targets for a savvy local boy, and when I see ladies pushing prams with their purses sitting on top, I think up a trick. I deliberately throw my towel in their direction so it lands on top of the purse, taking care to make it look like an accident. Then I apologise profusely and pick up my towel, scooping up the purse underneath and running off to the harbour, where I take out the money and throw the purse into the sea.

I also start shoplifting. I stroll into a shop with a towel around my neck, pick up a huge box of Maltesers and wrap it in the towel, and walk out. But before long I get caught, and the local bobby gives me a slap on the wrist and frogmarches me home. I get into a lot of trouble with Pete that day – he smacks me about and calls me a lowlife.

This turns out not to be my last encounter with the police. I carry on breaking and entering, and keep on getting caught. They threaten to send me to the juvenile court, but they never do. I get a thrill out of stealing, and even when I get a slap from the policeman, as well as from Pete, it feels good being noticed.

However, my wild streak is becoming more and more extreme. When I make money from shoplifting, I inevitably gamble it all away within a day or two. Then I stumble across the penny arcade on the seafront at Mevagissey. We have pockets full of tuppenny pieces, so I put them in to a game called Octopush – it feels like too good an opportunity to miss. Soon Kevin and I start banging the machine to make the coins fall out without anyone noticing. One evening, when I'm down to my last couple of tuppences and hungry as hell, I give the machine an almighty wallop – and the door holding all the pennies falls right open! I stare inside, my eyes wide and my mouth hanging open in astonishment – there are hundreds of pennies right within reach. Kevin and I stuff our pockets with them, and dash off to buy fish and chips and chocolate and fizzy drinks. We stuff ourselves silly, but soon there's a tap on our shoulder and we're dragged back home by the scruff of the neck once more.

"What would you rather have Rex, another brother or a little sister?"

Margaret is smiling at me across the kitchen table. For the first time in a while, I'm feeling excited at the prospect of having another sibling, probably because they will fill the gap that Bruce has left.

"A girl!" I exclaim, excited about a baby sister bringing something new and exciting to the family. I like the idea of having a baby around – someone to play with and to involve in our mischief when she's a bit older. And sure enough, Margaret does have a girl. She and Pete name her Caroline and I look forward to the adventures we'll have together. It's only then that I begin to forget about not knowing who my real mother is or what's happened to her.

Bruce comes home from Alex and Ida's, and it looks like he might be staying for a while. It's tough at first – he and

Pete have a huge fight, which ends with Pete putting his arm through the glass in the back door and cutting himself badly. The mood stays sour for days and Kevin and I feel like the piggies in the middle, left to pick up the pieces.

But despite this, I'm excited about our new life. The next few months are noisy and chaotic and difficult, but I sense that in the coming years we will rediscover the paradise that Rose Cottage is. So one day, when Pete comes to our bedroom to tell me and Kevin that there's a lady downstairs to see us, it doesn't occur to me that Margaret and Pete might be feeling differently about our situation. I'm so caught up in my feelings about mending our family and living a happy life together that when this stranger called Dorothy comes to talk to me about my school project on Australia and asks me whether I'd like to go and live in a country full of oranges and sunshine, I don't know what to say.

5.

A NEW CHAPTER

Bruce sarcastically tells us that Margaret's got more important things to think about than us now that she has Caroline, and that this is the perfect excuse for Pete to get rid of us. They are a proper family, and we're not a part of it. None of us wants to be taken away from Margaret and the life we've known until now – we love the woods and the freedom to roam around town like the feral children we've always been.

But one day in August 1970, a car arrives at the house to take us away. When she came to see us, Dorothy said they wouldn't dream of splitting up families, but Bruce doesn't come with us – he stays with Margaret and Pete, and we are told that another car will be coming to take him somewhere else in a few days. Our fragile family has been split up for good.

Two adults I've never seen before take Kevin and me on a long drive to the north coast of Cornwall, to Towan Blystra Children's Home in Newquay. On arrival, we are given injections to protect us against polio and other illnesses. On the outside we are loud and boisterous and push the other kids around, but on the inside I feel sore and rejected. Being sent to a children's home after five years of life at Mevagissey is very hard to come to terms with. Poor Kevin feels caught in the crossfire – whatever happens to me, he gets dragged along with it.

They have a television at the children's home so finally, at the age of 10, I get to see what I was missing out on in Mevagissey – and to be honest, I don't feel like I missed all that much! To me, it's just a flickering box full of crazy music and bright lights; I gather that the programme we're watching is *Top of the Pops*, but I find it hard to understand what's going on. I've never watched TV before, and it suddenly strikes me that living out in the middle of nowhere has meant that a lot of the music and fashion that fascinates the rest of the country has completely passed us by. The novelty of television is a welcome distraction though, and for the first time in my life, I have money to spend – every Saturday we get four shillings of pocket money.

I don't know the names of any other children in the home, so Kevin and I stick together. The place is run by a lady known as Auntie Mack, a slim, dark-haired woman with glasses. She is stern, but she doesn't hit us and we like her. Then there is Auntie Mary, a rotund lady with white hair, who is very funny.

Lots of shops have cigarette machines outside them, and they catch my eye when we go out to spend our pocket money at the weekends. I put in 10p and out comes a packet of five Woodbines. I dip into the shop and sneak out a lighter, and then I smoke my first cigarette on the beach on my own. It makes me splutter and cough, but I keep puffing. Smoking isn't allowed in the home, but doing things I'm not supposed to makes me feel independent, like I'm taking my life back into my own hands. I don't buy cigarettes from the machine every day, but I do start to make a habit out of it.

"Are you bloody smoking again, Rex?" Auntie Mary is sitting in a deckchair on the beach and reading the paper. How does she know I've smoked before, when I've never been caught?

"Put it out right now and come over here. You know very well it's not allowed, and it's bloody obvious what you've been doing when you turn up on the doorstep with that stink all over you." She gets up, grabs me by the wrist, and whisks me back to the home. I'm not allowed out for the next two weekends. It's miserable staying indoors while Kevin and all the others go out and enjoy themselves, but Auntie Mack and Auntie Mary still give me my pocket money each week.

"You're grounded, Rex, but we're not taking your money – that wouldn't be right. So you can save it up and spend it on something useful in two weeks' time."

This means that when I am allowed out again I have 12 shillings to spend and, sure enough, I immediately buy more cigarettes, as well as a couple of cap guns for good measure. When I get back, Kevin and I go to the graveyard opposite the home and start shooting at each other with them – much to the annoyance of the vicar, who storms out of the church and bellows at us.

To escape further punishment, I run down to the seaside and light up a cigarette. But who should be sitting there in a deckchair? Yes, it's Auntie Mary again!

But the fact is, they never hit me in the home – I'm doing all the hitting. Because I've been brought up with violence, it's like I don't know any other way of being. Pete was violent to me and so were the kids at school, so even though I don't feel that being violent is the "real me", it's a natural reaction to the violent world I was raised in. I'm just trying to protect myself from those around me, but I end up taking out my anger at Margaret and Pete's rejection of us on other people.

The sad thing is that this violent streak clouds my real interests – in things like nature, animals, and our outdoor games. For some reason, sometimes when I'm talking to the other children, I just snap and attack them, before apologising and carrying on as if nothing has happened. When I see them the next day, they run away from me. I just want to make friends, but I don't think I know how to. I never learned that at school.

"Tomorrow," Auntie Mary says, "you'll be going to London for a night or two. We've got some important people for you to meet, and then you'll be going on an adventure."

I do like adventures, but it seems strange to be going on one in the middle of December. What's more, I've learned to become suspicious when adults make plans without telling us what they are. Kevin looks uncertain too, but we can't argue, and the following day Auntie Mary takes us to the train station.

"Rex and Kevin, I've arranged a little surprise for you when we get to the station."

We both squirm in our seats. What now?

It's Bruce – he's come to say goodbye and to wave us off. He's just turned 16 and is wearing military uniform – he tells us that he's joined the army. Kevin and I don't really know what to say to him: our lives have grown further and further apart from his and we can't understand why he's allowed to join the army when we can't even decide whether we want to stay in Cornwall.

Bruce waves goodbye to us from the platform as the train pulls away. I feel angry that he's getting the opportunity to stay at home while we're being put on a train to who knows where. Little do we know that we won't see him again for 22 years.

The train ride is long and Kevin and I feel tense, because we don't know where we're going, or why. When we finally arrive in London, the city is enormous and grey and noisy. My eyes are out on stalks as we are walked briskly through the bustling streets teeming with Christmas shoppers. We are taken to a place called Bush House. We are disorientated and confused but also excited at this new adventure.

"Australia is a beautiful place at this time of year. Believe it or not, it's summer there right now!"

Of course I know this already, but it still seems like an amazing thought in the middle of a long, grey British winter. The lady on the other side of the desk – I think it's Dorothy again, the lady who came to see us at Rose Cottage – is leaning forward and smiling enthusiastically.

"And you'll see all sorts of amazing animals, Rex. I know you'll like them. There are kangaroos jumping about and wallabies everywhere – who knows, maybe you'll even ride horses to school!"

My jaw drops and Kevin stares at the lady, enthralled. Australia sounds like the most amazing place in the world, and we're being given the chance to go there to start a new life. Suddenly, we don't care about Cornwall anymore – all we want is to get on that plane right away. Life in the sunshine, surrounded by orange trees and exotic wildlife, sounds far better than getting thrashings from Pete every day.

"The place you're going to is in Tasmania, which is this island here in the south east." She points at a little triangle shape in the corner of the map. "It's called Tresca, near a town called Exeter – just like Exeter in Devon!"

The name Tresca conjures up an exotic array of images and we're thrilled at the prospect of an exciting new home, with horses and kangaroos everywhere.

"Fairbridge – that's us – already has everything organised. Margaret's parents have kindly said that you can stay with them tonight, and we've arranged a flight for you the day after tomorrow! Isn't that wonderful – you'll be out in Australia in just a few days – aren't you lucky!" By this point, Kevin and I are practically leaping out of our chairs with excitement.

The lady gives us each an identical blue suitcase packed with new clothes that they say have been bought specially for our journey. Then Ida and Alex come and take us back to West Wickham for the night. We don't get to sleep for ages, because we can't stop thinking about how wonderful our new life is going to be.

In the morning, they take us to a massive department store in the West End of London and buy me a boomerang that's being demonstrated in the shop. In the afternoon, we drive back to Kent and spend the rest of the day climbing the enormous tree at the far end of Ida and Alex's huge back garden. Ida and Alex tell us to pack up our bags before we go to bed, and give us each a new watch – we're being treated so well that we feel like royalty. The following morning – 10 December 1970 – we're taken back to the offices in London, where we're introduced to a couple who will accompany us on the flight to Tasmania, and they take us on to Heathrow Airport. Our adventure is about to begin.

PART II

TASMANIA

6.

TRESCA

We stop off in Singapore on the way. The couple who are accompanying us don't talk to us much. With the last of my pocket money that I saved from the home in Cornwall, I buy myself an Australian flag and a model plane – a German Stuka dive-bomber. I tear the plane from its packaging and spend the next few hours making dive-bomb noises.

"Yoooowwww! Bang! Yoooowwww! Bang!"

From Singapore we fly on to Sydney, and after another long wait we transfer to a small cylindrical aeroplane. "It looks like a cigar!" I shout, and Kevin doubles over with laughter as I hold my toy plane to my lips and pretend to smoke it.

The cigar plane takes us over the Bass Strait between mainland Australia and Tasmania, and we land at Launceston Airport. The plane stops on the tarmac some distance from the terminal building, and the attendant opens the doors and puts down the steps.

I look out from our window seats and see a man and a woman standing outside the terminal, waiting for us. She is skinny and he is balding and well built, a bit like Pete. Instinctively I feel wary of him, and I turn to Kevin and say, "I don't like them."

We step out into the scorching sun and are escorted across to the terminal to meet the new couple. The people who have accompanied us from London say goodbye and turn to go – and that's the last we see of them.

The man steps forward. "Hello boys. I'm Harry Richmond. Pleased to meet you. This is my wife Lily. We run the children's home in Tresca. Your mam and I are very pleased to have you."

Neither Kevin nor I say a word. We don't have a "mam" – we've never even had a mother, and there's no way we're going to start calling this woman that.

Harry and Lily take us through the terminal to an estate car that has three other lads sitting in it. We squeeze in, five kids and two adults all rammed into one car. There's a bench seat in the front, so one of the other boys sits there between Harry and Lily. Kevin sits in the middle with the other two and I'm put in the boot with our two suitcases, where I sit clutching my dive-bomber.

The other boys are brothers, too. Andrew Jones, the eldest, has a tough look about him, while his brothers Paul and Gary are non-identical twins. Paul is solidly built but Gary looks like a stick insect. To my surprise, they have English accents, and it turns out that they're from Yorkshire. That's not what I expected, and it suddenly feels like we've barely left home at all. But the heat tells me otherwise – it's scorching outside and we're sweating into our seats within minutes. I'm not sure whether the other boys have been waiting in the car all this time, but it must have been pretty uncomfortable if they were. December is only the start of the Australian summer, but the temperature is higher than we have ever experienced in Cornwall.

Harry and Lily try to chat to us on the way, but I'm not really in the mood for talking. *Your mam and I are very pleased to have you.* I'm boiling on the inside as well as the outside. Harry seems to think he and Lily are now our parents – just like that. But if he thinks we're going to act like their well-behaved kids, they've got another think coming. I will fight against that with all my might. He could easily have said something like, "we're going to look after you," but to try and pretend right from the beginning that we're their sons churns my stomach.

The drive from Launceston to the small town of Exeter is about 15 miles. It's a beautiful drive along the Tamar River, which we see glimpses of every now and again as the road nears it and then bends away again. Some of the place names are familiar, and I realise that a lot of them are the names of places in the West Country: there is a Tamar River in England, which neatly divides Devon and Cornwall; Launceston, where we landed, is a Cornish town on the Tamar; Exeter, of course, is also in Devon. But the lush vegetation and gum trees, the smells that came through the windows, and the sounds of unfamiliar birds are all very different from England. They are exactly what we dreamed about when we were told we would be coming here.

Exeter in Tasmania is a much smaller place than Exeter in Devon, with just a few hundred people living there. On the outskirts of the town, we turn left through pillared gates down a narrow road. There are fields on either side that turn into a golf course, with a row of pine trees that separate the road from the fairway and the green. After a couple of hundred yards, the road forks. To the right, a path leads straight up to the clubhouse, but we turn left and drive another hundred metres or so, before stopping with a crunch of gravel.

"Well, here we are, boys – welcome to Tresca!"

I feel dwarfed by the building looming over us out of the car window. There's a teardrop island of lawn with a single tree on it and a gravel driveway all around it, and to the right there's an aviary and a garage. In the middle of all this, painted white and towering above me with big white wooden columns and balustrades, is the house. It is old and built mainly of wood but has a green metal roof, punctured by three brick chimneys. Harry gets out and opens the doors for the boys in the middle. When he unloads the cases, I jump out after them. As I stand on the gravel clutching my Stuka dive-bomber in one sweaty hand, a blast of petrol fumes nearly knocks me over. Harry sees me wrinkle my nose and laughs.

"That's the fuel drum in the garage," he chuckles. "Most people decant their own fuel here, because lots of places are so remote. Those things can carry 44 gallons."

I stare up at the house and see a porch overhanging three or four wide wooden steps, leading to a large veranda that wraps around half of the building, with white balustrades and polished wooden floorboards. In the far corner there is a polished table – everywhere there is polish, polish,

polish. I tentatively walk up the steps onto the veranda and step through the door, from bright sun into suffocating darkness. There is no air inside and I can barely breathe.

I find myself in a sort of boot room and go through another door. A long corridor leads off to the right, while another opens up straight ahead. Harry leads us on, down to the end of the corridor and we turn right at the end, into a dormitory.

"This is your room, which you'll be sharing with Andrew. I'll just pop your cases on your beds, and then I'll take you for the tour, shall I?"

The dormitory has polished wooden floors, polished wooden beds and wooden dressing tables with mirrors. There are three windows, each higher than Kevin or I can reach, and two single beds on either side of the room.

Harry leads us out of the room and back up the corridor. On the left is another dormitory with three beds, where Paul and Gary sleep. Everything is made of the same meticulously polished wood. The décor in that dormitory is exactly the same as in ours: very clean, but stark, simple and not at all homely.

I have spent all my childhood – or all that I remember – in a beautiful old country cottage that felt like a family home, but this is glaringly cold and clinical and has none of that warmth. There are no pictures on the wall, apart from a portrait of the Queen at the end of the corridor. Harry nods at it as we walk past.

"You'll take it in turns to dust Her Majesty's portrait every day," he says.

Every *day*?

We pass a flight of stairs, and I crane my neck to see what's at the top of them.

"You mustn't go up there," Harry says firmly. "That's out of bounds."

Harry and Lily's bedroom is also on the ground floor – but unlike most of the other rooms, it is carpeted and has a low ceiling. There is also an office, a playroom, a lounge and a dining room – it is the largest house I've ever been in.

A hatch connects the dining room to the kitchen, where there is an Aga and a sink and cupboard units on the wall. Absolutely everything is painted aqua blue, and each of the doors has a little circular window cut into it, covered by wire mesh, which Harry says is for ventilation.

Beyond the Aga there is a tiny laundry room, and I can hear a low scrabbling sound coming from under the door.

"Kevin, Rex, time for you to meet Smudge and Gilligan," Harry grins. My heart skips a beat. Dogs!

He opens the door. Smudge and Gilligan scramble out and bundle around us, yapping noisily and nipping at our ankles. I feel an instant aversion to them, which I've never felt towards animals before.

Connected to the laundry room is a scullery, where there are bowls and plates in wall-mounted racks, as well as cutlery and cleaning gear. A frosted glass door leads out onto a little path that winds all the way round the house.

Harry and Lily have their own bathroom and we share the other – there are two stools, two showers and two sinks between five of us. The bathroom is painted red to knee height, and white above. The shower stalls are made of concrete, with wooden duckboards in each one. There is another shower room and a third dormitory with five beds, but that is out of bounds.

The house gives me a bad feeling: it's dark, gloomy, airless, and not at all like the people in London told me it would be. The dormitory feels horrible – I might as well be sleeping in a graveyard.

I wake up the next morning, excited to unpack my new blue suitcase and wear my new clothes. But our cases aren't where we left them the previous evening. Kevin and I search all over the room and under our beds, but they are nowhere to be seen – we can't even find the clothes we were wearing yesterday. Instead, we each find a pair of long shorts folded on a chair, along with checked shirts with long, pointed collars.

Harry marches in. "Ready for the run, boys?"

Kevin and I look at him, confused. What run?

"Where are our clothes?" Kevin asks. He looks like a little cowboy in his oversized shirt.

"Fresh start, boys! New life, new clothes," he barks, like some sort of military commander. We realise that he's taken our clothes — which were actually new, not made of itchy old cloth like these shorts — but he deliberately ignores us. He thinks we belong to him now, and that he can dress us and treat us how he wants. I grit my teeth.

Harry leads us outside. "Three laps around the house — follow the path. Good for the soul. We do this every day at the same time, rain or shine!"

By "we" he clearly means "you", because as soon as we set off, Harry retreats inside to his office and sits at his desk, watching us out of the window and making sure we all pass him three times. We pant and sweat in the morning sun and come indoors for breakfast already exhausted.

We have to adapt quickly to life in Tresca. There's a strict routine and we're made to follow it every day. After we come in from the morning run, the chores begin. After each meal, two of us have to go into the scullery and scrub the cutlery and crockery until they're sparkling. Reaching the plate racks high above my head is precarious, and I'm scared of what'll happen if I slip and break something. Other boys are assigned to polish all the wooden surfaces on the veranda or to clear Harry and Lily's room.

There are endless rules, and they all reflect Harry's obsession with cleanliness and order. Every time you have a shower you have to scrub the duckboard afterwards, which is less than relaxing in a steam-filled bathroom and makes you work up a sweat again immediately after washing. And every time we answer the phone, we have to say our number into the receiver before we say anything else: 003944371, a number that will stick in my head for a long time to come.

The Jones boys warn us that if we step out of line, we'll be severely beaten.

The day after we arrive, I'm having a breather in the playroom and it's boiling hot outside. Harry comes in and punches me jokingly on the arm. "Are you alright, son?" he asks. He sounds just like Pete, and it makes me shiver.

"I'm not your son," I snap back. And I run off. I run and run – out of the playroom, out of the door, down the steps, and down the road towards the golf course. At the fork in the road, I turn towards the clubhouse. There's no one there, so I decide to break in. I steal sweets and drinks and dash out again to gorge on them outside. Strangely, it's a long time before anyone comes looking for me. Even though I'm not far away, it's a few hours before Lily comes round the corner, spots me and takes me by the arm. I prepare myself for a beating, but she merely tells Harry, "He had a bit of a wobble," and that's the end of it.

But that isn't the end of it for me, because I don't want to be their child. I don't want to be indoctrinated into calling them mum and dad – I don't have a mum and dad, or if I do, I don't know who they are or whether they're alive or dead.

Margaret is the only person I'll ever consider anything like a real parent, so why couldn't I stay in Cornwall with her? I've come to the other side of the world and have been put in a house I don't like in the hands of total strangers. I will not let them have authority over me – why should I? They are not my parents, they cannot give me love, and they have no right to tell me what to do.

I soon realise the full extent of what I've got into: life at Tresca is a brutal regime, and I would far rather be in a home for "bad children" than here. The chores vary from week to week. Sometimes I find myself on my knees, cleaning the dirt out of the carpets with a hand brush. At other times I might be on kitchen duty, or cleaning the toilets and bathrooms. We have to do these chores before school in the morning, and if we don't finish them, we have to carry on as soon as we get home from school, before we start our homework. To me, especially after living in Heligan Woods and having the run of the town in Newquay, it is a crushingly cramped existence: chores, then school, then chores. If I'm late for school because of my chores (and of course, we don't ride horses to school, like the woman in London said we could), my teachers punish me and notify Harry, who then punishes me with even more chores. Or he takes away my privileges – not that we really have any in the first place.

Harry says he's "instilling discipline in you unruly boys", and that we'll thank him for it when we're grown up and successful. Some of the boys at school say my parents sound very strict, but I have no one to compare them with. And anyway, they're not my parents, so they can't order me to do anything. I refuse to call them mum and dad, and if he ever calls me "son" my response is always the same: "You're not my dad."

I stop calling him anything. Not "Harry", not "sir". Nothing. If he calls me, I just say, "Yes?"

Behind his back, though, we all call him "bastard". I never hear the Jones boys call them mum and dad, either – the three of them also dislike Harry and Lily, and want to get out of here as soon as they can. We often hatch plans to run away together. We reckon we could survive – Andrew and I are tough enough to protect the five of us, though I'm the toughest, really. He's a town boy and I was brought up in the woods – and no matter what anyone says, country kids are tougher than town kids. But we can never bring ourselves to run away properly: we don't know anything about our new world beyond school and Tresca, so we wouldn't have any idea where to go. Gary – the brainbox out of the five of us – doesn't do things without thinking them through properly first. While Andrew and I are busy plotting our escape routes, he's thinking carefully about what we'll need to survive in the bush. That doesn't occur to me – all I think about is the running away part, not what might happen afterwards.

There are some redeeming features about Tresca. The most obvious one is the grounds, which are huge and wild. We're sandwiched between the golf course and the bush, and there's a wooded hill rising above the house – in a way it reminds me of the magic of Rose Cottage. It's quiet and isolated and there's lots of nature, but it is mostly unfamiliar, which makes it all the more fascinating. The air smells of eucalyptus and in the heat of the summer, everything is so dry that the grass cracks underfoot as we walk on it. We hear the kookaburras in the mornings and the cacophony of cockatoos as they come in to roost in the evenings. Green parakeets dart around, in dramatic streaks of sound and colour. And in the bush around Tresca there are all kinds of animals I have never seen before, like wallabies, bandicoots, wombats, and snakes. And there are also terrifying new insects to deal with, like jack jumpers – a type of ant that can leap up from the ground and latch onto you – and the inchman, another type of ant that bites and never lets go.

All this is amazing to me, and my love of wildlife distracts me from the restrictions imposed on us for a little while. But we are still limited as to where we can go. There's a large expanse of grass around Tresca, but Harry only mows a small part of it and we're only allowed to play within the mown area. Sometimes we find goannas – a type of lizard – chopped clean in half by the lawn mower. Harry tells us that we mustn't go into the longer grass, because there's a ground-nesting bird called a plover that has spurs on its wings – apparently their behaviour is very aggressive when they have eggs and young in their nests, and the spurs could inject us with poison. We see them dive-bombing cats, dogs, lizards, and other birds, and believe Harry that the spurs are poisonous, even though he says it with a curious smile that doesn't quite look sincere.

Kevin and I miss our old freedom: we used to be able to roam far and wide, but Harry likes to keep us where he can see us — the little area of mown grass is right outside his office so that he can watch us from his desk. Whenever we disappear from his sight, he jumps up from his desk, rushes outside and yells at us. It makes me boil inside. He seems to think we belong to him and don't deserve any independence of our own, so naturally I run off into the bush whenever I can. I particularly like to run up the hill into the woods, where it's wild and reminds me of home.

7.

POMS AND CRIMINALS

"Walking to school is good for you, boys. A bit of exercise will set you up for the day. Now you fellas have a good day, and I'll see you later."

Andrew turns to me surreptitiously. "Get used to this – the bastard never drives us to school or picks us up, even if it's pouring."

We start school almost immediately after our arrival in Tasmania, the week before it closes for Christmas. Andrew, Gary and Paul lead the way down the long drive to the main road, past the golf course.

"It'd be quickest to cut across the fairway," says Gary, "but Harry would slaughter us if we got caught."

It's a long walk to Exeter District School, which is on a road called Glen-Ard-Mohr. The name makes me think of

Scotland, even though I've never been there and have no idea what it's like. The school is much bigger than the one in Mevagissey, and the kids there come from the country farmsteads all around Exeter. In many respects it's just like the other schools I've been to: nondescript single-storey buildings, full of endless corridors.

On my first day, my new classmates ask me the usual questions about where I'm from. When they realise I'm different they say things like, "Hey, Rex, have you been to Tatana?"

"No, Exeter's the only place I've been in Tasmania," I say, and they fall about laughing. I don't know why, and feel like I'm back in the playground with Ant Miller all over again. Anger surges inside me.

"It's the same thing, mate. Tatana is the aboriginal name for Exeter. But you wouldn't know that, would you, you Pommie bastard."

And so it starts all over again. They tease us relentlessly, calling us "Poms", which Andrew tells me means "prisoners of mother England." It starts off as banter, and doesn't really mean anything more serious or nasty. But calling me a "Pom" makes me understand that I am different to all the others, and will be treated accordingly. Bullying always starts like that – it's just like when I was the kid from the woods in Mevagissey. On day one they isolate me, then within weeks they start roughing me up and calling me worse names.

When I find myself cornered and the local boys are taunting me, I spit back at them, "It's not me that's the prisoner of mother England, it was your great-grandfather. You're not even Australian. Your family were criminals. You're only here because your great-grandad stole a loaf of bread in Bristol."

They rise to it, and there are more of them than me. Soon I'm getting kicks and punches in the playground and coming home battered and bruised on a regular basis. But I do my best to show them that they're messing with the wrong kid. I'm not the kind of person to just roll over and accept it anymore. I've been bullied and I've been a bully, so I know how it goes. My life has made me violent and streetwise.

In reality, though, it cuts me deep when they call me a "prisoner of mother England", because I know that's exactly what I am. It's not them who have been transported to the other side of the world by a bunch of establishment English colonialists and locked up in a virtual prison. It's me.

My classroom is two doors down from the tuckshop, where I go at lunchtimes to buy vegemite and lettuce or banana and honey sandwiches, wrapped in greaseproof paper. My teacher, Mrs Ealey, is a fearsome woman – she's a young mother and is hard as nails.

I sit at the back of the class every day and refuse to listen to a thing they're trying to teach us. I'm fed up of being a Pom and an outcast, and I'm fed up of school. I sit there drawing pin men fighting one another and tanks and stuff. I stay at it for hours, and my head is not in the classroom. It is out in Heligan Woods with the deer and the owls, or it is up the hill away from Tresca with the kookaburras and the cockatoos. I'm not an indoors person. I spend every hour inside thinking about what I could be doing outside.

"Let's remind ourselves of what we talked about last lesson. What did we learn yesterday, Rex?"

Mrs Ealey fixes me with her stern gaze. I don't even look up from my drawings. What did we learn yesterday? I was doing my drawings then, too.

So I tell her the truth.

"I wasn't listening."

I flick my pencil and the armed man on the right shoots the stick man on the left clean through the head. The next thing I know, a firm hand clamps round my jaw and drags me up off my chair, out of the classroom and down the aisle, all the way to the headmaster's office.

"Sir, Wilton here is not only refusing to learn, but he's also being unacceptably rude to me in my own classroom," Mrs Ealey barks.

"Is that right? Anything to say for yourself, Wilton?"

I stare him in the eye defiantly and say nothing.

"Nothing?"

I glare at him.

"You leave me with no choice, Wilton – not learning in school is bad enough, but insulting your teachers is a different matter altogether. Six of the best for you." My first encounter with the headmaster is swift and painful, and it won't be the last time I feel his wrath.

The only really good thing about Exeter District School is my science teacher, a man called Noel Perks. He's absolutely fantastic and is the one person who actually encourages me rather than beating me and punishing me. For the first time, I come to know and respect an adult man who isn't obsessed with iron discipline and violence.

After a while, I meet some other lovely people at school and I finally begin to feel accepted for who I am. They don't care that I'm a Pom. I fell in with the wrong crowd at first, but no more. I meet a man mountain outside class and ready myself for a fight, but then he introduces himself: "Jason Brocklehurst. Nice to meet you, mate. This is my sister, Gloria." I stare at her. She is gorgeous, with tight white curly hair. Jason seems as gentle as anything, despite his size, but I'm still suspicious of him. I don't know what to say to them, but still expect him to start shoving me about and calling me names – so instinctively I go on the attack and call his sister a Golliwog. They both look hurt, but I feel more powerful for delivering the first blow.

I can't stop looking at Gloria or thinking about her, but I don't know how to get her attention except by being mean to her. Any opportunity to hurt people makes me feel more in control and less of an outsider, even though I feel bad about it later and can't explain why I'm nasty to Gloria, when I like her. And the others at school start picking on me because I pick on her.

But Jason seems to understand; he's kind to me and never calls me names, and Gloria seems to forgive me, too. Eventually I learn to treat them as I want them to treat me, and we become friends. I spend all my time at school with them if I can. The first time Gloria invites me to their house, I can barely contain my excitement. I run home as fast as I can and dash into Harry's office, red-faced and bright-eyed and panting. Harry is sitting at his desk, and looks up nonchalantly.

"Please can I go to my friends' house tomorrow after school?"

He looks at me for a moment. "Rex, the shower was in a bit of a state when you left this morning. Don't you think you've got some work to do?"

I stumble over my words. "But… please can I go after school tomorrow?"

"Rex, you know you're not allowed to go to other people's houses after school when there are jobs that need doing here. This house can't run itself. Lily and I work very hard to provide for you boys, but we need you to finish your chores."

My heart sinks. The following day I avoid Jason and Gloria because I'm too ashamed to tell them I'm not allowed the freedom that everyone else has. That afternoon I trudge home despondently and polish the skirting boards on the veranda, gazing wistfully out towards the woods on the hill.

In the morning, Gloria finds me before class begins.

She looks disappointed. "I thought you were going to come to my house," she says. I feel terrible – like I'm wasting the only true friendships I've got. Most of all, I feel embarrassed that I'm not a normal kid.

"Oh, I had to… I had to go somewhere else," I mumble lamely. I look up at her with sad eyes and I can't tell whether she understands.

8.

RUN

I hate Harry and Lily for stopping me making real friends, so I take every chance to get back at them. Harry gets me new shoes to wear school, and I despise them more than anything: they're made of stiff, creaky leather and are polished to within an inch of their life. I've never liked wearing shoes, so I find ways to wear them down until they've got a hole in them and Harry has to throw them away. I get Jason to pull me over the surface of the playground just to wear them out.

I don't think Harry and Lily have ever had children of their own. I know they came over from England before I was born, but I don't know anything about their lives before arriving in Tasmania. They took charge of Tresca in 1958 and lots of other kids have stayed there, so I think they should know how to treat us better. They want us to call them mum and dad, but they're nothing like how I'd want my real parents to be. Harry is cold and distant, and if I hurt myself, neither he nor Lily shows me any tenderness.

And sometimes it's them doing the hurting. If we haven't finished our chores Harry threatens us, saying, "I'll go to town on you." That's when we know we're at risk of a good hiding. If we're late or untidy or he thinks we've done a chore badly, we get smacked or thumped or cuffed.

We're all treated the same at Tresca, but one thing is for sure: I don't see any love or kindness. From the outside, it probably looks more like they're running a business – some kind of depraved polishing business that employs children round the clock for free. All they seem to care about is projecting an image of being good and responsible parents, but our shiny shoes conceal the neglect that we suffer from the outside world.

At Tresca, we are forced to go to church every Sunday, though I don't know if I believe any of what we are told there. We're given 40 cents a week pocket money, of which 10 cents has to go in our moneyboxes and 20 cents into the church collection. I usually blow most of the money at school on Monday, but if I don't have any left for church on Sunday, I have to give double the following weekend.

And because that's often the case, I start stealing money – to put in the church collection. I have no choice!

Eventually I'm put in charge of counting the collection money – who knows why they let me do it. Perhaps Harry and Lily sense that I'm not interested in church and want me to develop a sense of responsibility. Or perhaps they just want to show off their wonderful, well-behaved "good little Christian boys."

But I'm damned if I'm going to let an opportunity like that slide, so not all the collection money stays in the bowl. If we're going to be terrorised into going to church and coughing up half our pocket money on something we're not interested in, I'm going to get my own back. I can't do it by speaking up, because no one would listen. I can't say, "I got hit on the head by Harry last night," because no one would believe me. So my first response is to steal.

*

The phone rings and I pick it up.

"Hello, can I help?"

I don't even see the shovel. All of a sudden I'm face down on the floor with a searing pain in my chin and blood bursting from my bottom lip.

Lily is standing over me and shouting.

"You say the number first, you miserable child! How many times have we told you?"

I forgot to say the number. "003944371 – How can I help?" That is a mistake I will never make again.

The more violence I suffer at Harry and Lily's hands, the angrier and more vengeful I become. The next time I'm on cleaning duty in their bedroom, I rifle through Harry's trouser pockets, fish out a wad of banknotes, and take $50. Later that afternoon, I go to a shop in town, buy as many sweets as I can, and bring them back to Tresca to share with the others.

That afternoon, Harry's booming voice calls me to his office, and I know the game is up. I creep along the corridor to his room, expecting a severe talking to and a cuff about the head. But the moment I open the door my head hits the wall with tremendous force. He pins me against it, as Gilligan the corgi clamps his jaws down on my ankle. I howl in pain and anger and aim a desperate kick at the dog to try and get it off me. Harry sees this and bellows as he strikes me viciously on the temple, thrashing me until I can barely stand up. Thoroughly beaten, I show him my bleeding leg and ask for something to stop the blood. His lip curls as he looks down at me, utter contempt in his eyes, and shouts out, "Ma'am" – which is what he calls Lily in front of us.

Lily is as bad and as violent as Harry. She has a horrible screechy voice and I can't bear to be in the same room as her. It's even worse when she doesn't have her teeth in. Him yelling out "Ma'am" is her cue to come in and slap some iodine on the dog bite and put a bandage on. She shows no sympathy or care, but gives the impression that I deserve it. I know stealing is bad, but I only do it because they are horrible to me – and then they beat me until I bleed as punishment.

Kevin and I have to fumigate chairs with insecticide in the old aviary as one of our regular chores. Around two years after our arrival, a few days before Christmas, Harry strides into the aviary, stands over me and orders me to stop my work. He points at one of the geese in the aviary, and orders me to pick it up and come with him to the shed next door.

I follow him to the shed, cradling the peaceful goose in my arms, feeling the comforting warmth of its soft feathers against my skin. Harry turns to face me.

"Snap its neck, Rex."

I look at him with wide eyes. "No."

"What?"

"I don't want to snap its neck. I love geese."

"But I bet you'll bloody well eat it, won't you?"

"Yes."

"It's your Christmas dinner. So snap its neck."

"No."

He's right that I do like eating goose, but I haven't got the heart to kill it myself. So instead, he holds the goose down and forces me to watch as he wrings its neck in front of me.

"There, how hard was that?" he snaps, standing up and wiping his hands on his trousers. "Bloody coward you are, Wilton. Next time, you'll bloody well do as you're told."

Tears prickle in my eyes as he gives me a hiding and orders me to carry the dead goose into the house.

We do celebrate Christmas, Easter and birthdays at Tresca, but they're not much different from any other day. At Christmas we have a tree and a small Christmas dinner, but it feels joyless somehow, as though the main part of Christmas – being with the people you love most – is absent. I feel subdued, even on those special occasions. We're never allowed to invite friends round, even for birthdays – we have a cake and a card and that's it. At Easter we are each given a chocolate egg and told when we are allowed to eat it. In some ways it all sounds normal, but it feels like a token gesture, so that they can say to the local council or to the people who sent us here, "We celebrate Christmas with them, and we bake a cake for their birthdays." It's not as if we have to survive on bread and water, but we are impoverished in almost every other sense.

Violence and confinement are not the only problems at Tresca. As time goes on, Harry begins to rent us out – effectively as slave labour. One Saturday he announces that Kevin and I will be going to a farm at Beaconsfield for the day, and that if we're good we'll be able to go there every week. It may be an escape from Tresca, but it's hardly a holiday. Harry takes us there in the car and greets the farmer, who shows us round and tasks us with coating fence posts with sump oil and cutting thistles in the paddocks. Harry, meanwhile, stands around chatting to the farmer, before driving off back to Tresca.

On some occasions we're taken to the house of two old ladies who have an old black Wolseley car parked outside. We tidy for them and do various little other jobs around the house, cleaning windows and scrubbing floors. Before we leave, Kevin and I see the ladies hand over a couple of banknotes to Harry. But on the way home there's no mention of payment for us, and we don't receive any extra pocket money at the end of the week, either.

The other place they take us to is a little holiday cottage Harry and Lily have at Deviot, right next to the Tamar River. The river is wide and open there and it's a beautiful spot, but we spend most of our time cutting the grass, weeding and trimming hedges in the grounds. A number of times we injure ourselves on the garden tools.

What are we supposed to be – hired help, who never get paid? Who do they think we are? We're meant to be in their care, and yet they use us for labour, they never let us go to our friends' houses, they barely let us out of their sight, and they beat us if they think we've done something wrong. It's a borstal, not a home. We're not allowed to mix with our friends outside school and the only time we are taken to Launceston is to buy clothes. On those rare occasions, we are accompanied all the way: they decide on the itchy old materials to dress us in and stay with us the entire time.

I am beaten at home and I am beaten at school. It feels like there is no one who will listen to my worries and take me seriously. When Harry makes me take a heavy wheelbarrow up a grassy slope in the garden in the rain, I fall, split my tongue and chip a front tooth, but nobody bats an eyelid. Harry refuses even take me to the doctor. Every day on the way to school I hope that one of my teachers will notice that something is wrong, that the bruises appearing on my face and arms can't be getting there by accident.

But they don't notice, and I have nobody to tell. Harry is a member of the masons and the Rotary club, and he makes a big thing of it. When he beats me and I cry and shout that I'll tell someone about it, he reminds me of this, as if to say that if we tell anybody, they won't believe us – that they'll take his word over ours. And he's right.

Perhaps at some level Harry and Lily Richmond are concerned for our wellbeing, but I can't see myself ever being happy with them and I resent the things they make me do. So I step up my rebellion against them and run away whenever I can. When I disappear into the bush for a few days at a time, it feels like I'm reclaiming my freedom. I go on little walkabouts, roaming the woods and looking for wildlife, and when night falls I sneak into empty hay barns to sleep. Sometimes people from school find me and bring me food or a couple of dollars so that I can go and buy some bread. Or I simply bump into people and say, "I'm hungry" – and they give me food. I sometimes have to steal things – like milk from people's doorsteps – but on the whole, I'm surprised by people's generosity and the fact that so few people ask what I am doing out here.

I find an old mattress at the local dump and sleep on it for three days. My lust for freedom and adventure is finally satisfied – along with my penchant for mischief and, I suppose, a streak of something darker as well. My single aim is to get out of Tresca, because I hate Harry and Lily's pretence of being caring foster parents. I don't see a future in living in the wild, but I don't have anywhere else to go and at least if I get caught stealing, I won't have to go back to Tresca. Realistically, I'll probably end up in Ashley Home for Boys, a detention centre that is effectively a juvenile prison. But part of me thinks that if I'm going to be held against my will, I'd rather be in a prison than in a "family home" that isn't really any different. I don't want to be away from Kevin, but I want to be free. I'm still sad to be separated from Margaret, and even in Tasmania I often think about her and Rose Cottage, and Ida and Alex in Kent. I think back on my old life and feel upset that I've been taken away from the few people who really mattered to me and made me happy.

By the age of twelve I'm running away very frequently, and one day Harry finds me out in the bush. He beats me severely and tells me I've got to see a psychologist who will get to the bottom of what's wrong in my head.

*

"Why do you try to run away?"

"Because I hate it here."

"What do you hate about it?"

"I hate Harry and Lily and I hate the house and I don't want to be here."

"But Harry and Lily are just trying to give you a proper upbringing. You make their lives very difficult if you're always running away."

"They hurt me."

"What do you expect, if you're always stealing and running away?"

And on it goes – according to the psychologist, it's me that's the problem. They just need to find out what's wrong with me, and then the problem will go away. It's true that I am not well behaved and that I'm violent, but the only two significant male influences in my life, Pete and Harry, have taught me that violence is an acceptable response to lots of different situations. Between the two of them, they have infected me with a bad idea of what it means to be a man, and it will take many years to get rid of that.

The following week, the psychologist produces four model dogs and puts them on the table.

"This one is the mother. This is the father. This is the brother and this is the sister. Where do you fit in?"

I don't have a mum. I don't have a dad. I don't have a sister, and I don't have a bloody dog! I stare hard at him. "I'm a boy," I say.

"But how do you fit in to the family unit?"

He fails to realise that he's talking to someone who's never been part of one – I can't relate to four model dogs on a table, or to the idea of a family unit.

Week after week, it feels like the psychologists are just looking at my behaviour on the surface, rather than at the reasons for it. I've never known my mother and father, the only mother I've ever known got rid of me, I've been physically abused and taken thousands of miles round the world with one brother and nothing else, but they aren't thinking about any of that. They're just asking me why I want to run away – why am I so uncooperative? I want to know why I've been sent here and where Bruce and my mother are. But nobody else wants to help me find the answers.

The worst thing about running away from Tresca is leaving Kevin in the lurch. I'm always aware that I'm abandoning him, just like my parents abandoned us before. I want to be a responsible older brother, but the truth is that he probably has a wiser and more reasonable head on his shoulders than me. So while he's sensibly getting on with life at Tresca, I'm becoming ever more unreasonable. I feel horrible for Kevin, because I have become so swept up in my own problems that I am beginning to ignore him.

Each time I run away, I get further and further before I'm caught. Hitchhiking is common here and we always see hitchhikers on our way to school, so I copy them and stand by the roadside with my arm extended and my thumb up. The first time I do it, getting in a car with a stranger feels peculiar, but once I get over the initial awkwardness I stop worrying and start to make a habit of it. A lift is a lift and there's nothing to be scared of.

I'm walking up the main road towards Launceston with my back to the passing cars and my arm outstretched. It's the end of the Australian summer: the temperature is scorching and the road is dusty. I'm exhausted and dehydrated, and every car that passes without stopping brings a fresh wave of disappointment.

I hear a rumbling behind me and step slightly away from the road, but rather than overtaking me, the car slows to walking pace. For ten metres, I continue along the road with the car prowling behind me. Slightly unsettled, I look over my shoulder. The car is dark red and looks old, the metalwork rusted. It gently accelerates, pulls up alongside me and stops. A man leans across the passenger seat and speaks to me through the open window.

"Jump in, son. Where are you heading?"

"Launceston." I open the door and collapse into the seat, too tired to strike up any further conversation.

The man smiles at me and turns his attention back to the road. We carry on towards Launceston in silence, but from time to time he turns to look at me. At the edge of the town, he stops at a chemist and disappears into the shop for a while. The car has a musty smell and the heat is making me uncomfortable, but I'm desperate to get as far away as possible from Tresca and nothing else matters.

I don't know what he's bought in the chemist – he's not carrying a bag when he comes back and gets in. I wait for him to start the engine, but he sits still and stares at me.

"You're going to have do me a favour," he says, looking me in the eye. "I'll take you where you want to go, but I need something in return. It won't take long."

"I don't have any money," I say, despondent but defiant.

He laughs. "No problem. It's something else. No big deal."

He drives out of town again and stops the car in a remote spot that I don't recognise. Before I know what's happening, he grabs hold of me and shoves my face down into the back seat. I fight back, kicking out and biting at his arms, but I don't fight hard enough and he is too strong. He pins me down on my front. I gasp and shout and struggle for breath. He tugs at my clothes.

I don't know how long it lasts. The pain is like nothing I've ever known. When it's over, he drags me from the car and leaves me lying on the ground. I curl up in a ball, disgusted and furious with myself.

I hate myself for a long time afterwards. As much as I want to blame him, I hate myself for getting in his car. More than anything, I feel ashamed. I don't want to tell anyone, but a month or so later I am forced to. In the shower one morning, I discover a red lump on my groin, and soon it develops into an ugly boil. Eventually I tell Harry and he arranges for me to go to the doctor.

The doctor examines me and takes some tests, before looking at me severely and telling me that I have an STD. I don't know what that means, but when he explains, I feel utterly humiliated – it's like someone has discovered my dirty secret. With incredible difficulty, I tell him everything – how I ran away and got into a man's car, and what he did to me.

He looks on with an uninterested expression. "There's not much we can do about that, but we'd better get you fixed up."

The boil is treated and gradually gets less painful, but it soon becomes clear that no one is following up the crime – I suspect they assume I've made it all up. Or perhaps Harry knows and doesn't want the story of me running away into danger to get out.

It's around this time that I start stealing booze. I'm 14 years old and have hit rock bottom. I descend into a life of pilfering and bingeing. I can't afford alcohol, so I simply steal it from shops. Nobody guards the entrances, so when the shopkeeper's back is turned I have a clear run for the exit. I drink beer, Scotch and cider – whatever I can get my hands on. The alcohol numbs the pain of my past. All I can think about in the morning is my first drink – so I can escape the hideous memory of the man in the red car. I start getting so drunk that the following day I can't remember anything I've done. And I start to steal fags as well – they are right next to the checkout, so I can pocket a packet and stroll straight out of the door.

But my drinking gets me into trouble, and after a few incidents involving violence and vandalism, I get sent for a short stint in the Ashley Home for Boys. Harry comes to see me while I'm there and says something like, "We want to have you back, Rex, but you're going to have to start behaving yourself." I say sorry, mostly because I feel bad about abandoning Kevin, but also because I want to shut Harry up. I don't want to see him, and I'm furious with him for the way my life has turned out. But I start to feel guilty – it's like the rape has changed everything. Because all of a sudden I've begun to feel like it really is me that's the problem: I still feel disgusted with myself, and I'm doing things that I know are wrong and that will get me into trouble. At the same time, I don't care anymore, and the following months go by in a blurred, drunken haze.

9.

FIRE

I spend five years at Exeter District School, until my erratic behaviour tips over the edge and leaves them with no other option than to exclude me. It is 1975 and I am 16 years old, back at Tresca after spending some time at Ashley. Harry and Lily take us to a Fairbridge event held to congratulate them on their brilliant parenting skills, but all the backslapping and hearty laughter makes me angry and I'm desperate to get away from the disingenuous smiles of the men in suits from London. Fairbridge was supposed to have our best interests at heart, and yet neither this event nor the state of our lives suggests anything of the sort.

So, when backs are turned during yet another long speech excelling the virtues of my torturers, I sneak away. I'm not exactly sure where I'm going, but the event is not far from my school, so I naturally end up there. I hate my teachers for the authority they hold over me and their refusal to listen to me and help me, even when I'm being roughed up in class and at home. I know it'll be easy to break in to school this evening, because there are no alarms. So, with no plan other than to do some damage and get my own back, I put glue on the window and stick some paper to it, to prevent the glass flying everywhere. When I smash the window, it shatters quietly.

I'm in. What to do? First, I raid the tuckshop. I stuff myself and fill my pockets with snacks and goodies. Then I turn and head for the science lab, where I decide to do an experiment. I light a Bunsen burner and get out some ether. I'm fascinated see how flammable it is, so I pour some onto the table, and it flows along the workbench towards the Bunsen burner.

The liquid rapidly ignites with a brilliant flash, and all of a sudden there's a deafening explosion, as the flames reach the bottle and it bursts into a ball of fire. I panic and turn to run out of the lab, smashing straight into the door, which I thought I'd left open. I collapse on the floor, my head swimming. I bundle myself out through the doorway, as the flames lick the walls of the lab behind me. I stagger through the school and back out the same way I came in. As I reach the road, I cast a nervous glance round, and see that the centre of the school on fire. I run down Glen-Ard-Mohr Road, down a gravel track near the river and under the bridge, where I collapse in exhaustion.

That night, I sleep under the bridge while the school burns. I don't know how much damage has been done, but my sleep is broken by the wailing sirens of fire engines.

In the morning, I creep out from under the bridge and steal a loaf from someone's doorstep for my breakfast. As I round the corner in the next street, chewing on a mouthful of bread, my way is blocked by a towering policeman.

"Game's up, son. You're coming with me."

I have no defence, but also have no idea how he knows I'm responsible – perhaps someone saw me stealing the bread and alerted him.

In a daze, I am taken to the station, where unfamiliar faces throw around words like "arson" and "vandalism" and "charge". Then they send me off to the Ashley Home for Boys.

The bloke running the place is a stern man called Harry Laing. He tells me that if I toe the line I won't have any problems, but that if I don't I'll be in trouble.

Every day at Ashley, I have to polish my cell until it's sparkling and scrub the back steps with a toothbrush. If I step out of line I have my privileges taken away, so I have to get other inmates to sneak me cigarettes.

As the days blur into another depressing haze of chores and routine, I hit a brick wall. I am a 16-year-old kid in a child detention centre thousands of miles from where I was born. I've been excluded from school. My father is dead, my mother disappeared without a trace, and I don't think I'm ever going to see my big brother again. I'm not going to get any qualifications. I cannot sink any lower, and I have nothing to aim for.

So I decide to end it. There aren't many obvious ways to do it in the detention centre, but I decide that the easiest way is to drink weed-killer – we use it to spray the cracks between paving stones. People usually just leave it lying around when they've finished.

The following morning I'm out on cleaning duty. I get hold of a bottle of the stuff, hold it to my lips without giving it a second thought and take a big mouthful. The taste is viciously bitter and suffocating and makes me retch, but I screw my eyes shut and swallow it straight down.

But I don't hold my nerve to the end, and am immediately overwhelmed by a rush of guilt and anxiety. Clutching my stomach, I stagger down the corridor to find Harry Laing and tell him what I've done. He hurries me to a car and I'm rushed to hospital, where I remain critically ill for several days. It takes me some time to make a full recovery.

When I finish my sentence at Ashley, Exeter High School don't want to have me back, for some reason. So I move to Riverside High School, on the Tamar River between Exeter and Launceston. I'm lucky to get into Riverside on the back of what I did – it seems surprising to me that any school would accept a pupil who's just burned their previous school to the ground.

There's a teacher at Riverside who I dislike right from the beginning. He's a strange, pale man called Mr Best who stalks the corridors every day, wearing a peculiar long flowing robe, keeping an eye out for troublemakers. One day he catches me smoking, which means the standard punishment of four strokes across the palm of the hand with a cane. For some reason he gives me six, and then forces me to write out lines – a particularly sadistic punishment, as it's almost impossible to write when your hand has been slashed. So I call him a "silly old coot" and threaten to burn the school down. He takes it as a serious threat, of course, because I have already burned one school down.

This incident, among others, comes out at my arson trial, during which I learn that I my actions have caused $250,000 of damage. Not knowing how to justify my actions and raging at how I've been treated by Harry and Lily and my teachers at Exeter, I tell the judge that I'd planned to make a bomb to blow the doors off the school office, so I could steal money. I've got wind of the fact that Bruce is in the army in Germany, so I claim that I wanted to steal enough money to go there in search of him and my mum. I know that would have been a pretty stupid plan, because the office wouldn't have much money in it, but they buy it anyway.

My trial is reported in the local press:

YOUTH WANTED CHEMICALS TO MAKE BOMBS

A YOUTH charged with setting fire to the Exeter District School in August wanted to make bombs, the Launceston Supreme Court was told yesterday.

The youth (16) broke into the school to steal chemicals for this purpose, the Crown Prosecutor Mr M. Allen told the court.

Mr Allen was reading from a written statement the youth made to George Town police on the morning of the fire.

In the statement, the youth said that he had made Molotov cocktails in the past.

He claimed that he removed chemicals from the science block of the school, including a bottle of ether, which made him dizzy when he sniffed it.

While he was pouring the ether into a container, it exploded in his face, the statement said.

The headmaster of the school, Mr A. Rae, of Cormiston Rd, Riverside, said he was called to the school about 5am.

"I saw the school burning," he said.

The science room and adjoining classrooms were destroyed, along with equipment worth $10,000.

The trial before Mr Justice Crawford will resume today.

The judge decides to go easy on me, because he notes that I've lived "in institutions or quasi institutions all my life, and have never known a normal life." My lawyer says that I could and should be encouraged to live "a decent and honest life". That might be the case, but I'm certainly not ready for it yet. I wouldn't know how. I'm placed on two years' probation and am sent back to Riverside. The following year, at the age of 17, I leave school without any qualifications and head for Launceston, where I am given a place at the St Vincent de Paul Hostel.

From now on I am effectively an independent adult, though I don't feel equipped to look after myself properly. The next few years are going to be tough – but I don't yet realise just how tough they will be.

10.

A Life of Crime

The hostel is run by the St Vincent de Paul Society, a Catholic charity with branches all over the place. This one is an old cinema converted into a clothing store. They sell clothes in the foyer and in the back there's an old guy called Bert who makes rags from clothes that are not good enough to sell. He sits there with his blade for eight hours a day, filling bags with rags, and then goes off to hawk them to garages and other companies in the area. He lives in a little room off the main foyer and I talk to him a lot when I first arrive. He has worked here for yonks and is part of the furniture.

The accommodation block is next door to the store. It's meant to be a sort of halfway house between the detention centre and getting your own place. I'm still technically in state care until the age of 21, but the only contact I have with the authorities now is with my probation officer, who I have to check in with at regular intervals.

At Vinnie's (as everyone calls it) I am allocated a shared room with some totally religious bloke who spouts the Bible at me and prays every night. He really gets on my wick from day one. I'm full of rage and ready to take it out on the world, and here's a stranger lecturing me about forgiveness and turning the other cheek. I'm not going to take lessons from him or anybody else – I've had enough of authority and the pain it inflicts, and I'm certainly not going to accept the words of religion. Now, unconstrained by controlling foster parents or institutions, I can let my emotions loose.

But at the same time, I begin to look for answers. I've never been into religion as such: I'm more into what Dave Allen says – "may your God go with you" – but I do have my own personal beliefs, and I don't think I have to go to church to be a Christian. To me, the bloke I'm sharing with is all show.

Through St Vincent de Paul I meet a Catholic priest called Father Hugh Shearer at a local church called St Finn Barr's. He's totally different from any religious person I've met before: up to this point I've assumed that priests abstain from smoking and drinking, but he does both, and

I can relate to him. He is down-to-earth, and calls me "little brother". He gives me money when I don't have any. He gives me a room. And he never once lays a hand on me. He never pushes religion on me either, but I end up going to one of his services, simply because I like and respect him. The service is in Latin and I don't understand it, so I never go again, but I could not have met a nicer person.

Father Hugh encourages me to strive to do better. He gives me the impetus to carry on trying to understand my life, and that gives me a reason to carry on living. I am trying to find an answer to all the questions that are crashing around inside me – I've been to a few different churches, but I've never found one that I fit into. My philosophy is that you have to see it to believe it, and I don't feel that I've ever seen God, so I cannot believe that he's there. I'm not saying that I haven't taken part in services or that I haven't read the Bible, because I have. I do have a sense of there being something greater than my understanding – I've just never quite discovered what it is. And the truth is, I'm not ready to live a good life, because my upbringing has not taught me how. It has only taught me to distrust authority and to rebel – I've embarked not on a spiritual path, but on a life of petty crime and squalid drunkenness.

The St Vincent de Paul charity helps underprivileged people by giving them clothes and furniture, and I work in the delivery vehicles. I'm not paid a proper wage, because I'm on probation, but I do get an allowance, which means that I have money to buy alcohol and cigarettes. But I am also stealing again, to pay for other stuff.

I buy a .22 rifle. It's not a big deal to have one in Tasmania, but it inevitably gets me into trouble. The police arrest me and accuse me of shooting at a car coming down the main road. I did it because I wanted to test the rifle, so I shot vaguely in the direction of a passing car. I didn't do any damage, and nobody got hurt, but it was obviously a hugely dangerous and stupid thing to do. They search my room, find the rifle wrapped up in a rug, and arrest me. I am escorted to the police station. A huge plainclothes policeman called Phil clouts me round the back of the head with a phone book and I yell out in pain, so he responds by hitting me in the guts with it. I look at my rifle in the corner, and he goes to pick it up, before marching over to me and whacking me in the shin with the butt. "You're a bastard," he says. "A lying little shit." He goes at me good and proper, beating me and shouting abuse at me. I have a sore shin and my guts and head hurt, but I'm not taken to court – they confiscate the rifle, give me a final hiding and turf me out on the street. I don't know if it was illegal for me to own the gun, but I've learned not to fire it at cars again. I'm lucky that they accepted I wasn't trying to kill anyone. However, my experience at the station establishes a pattern of police brutality in my life, and I get to know the cops in Launceston quite well.

There's another incident with a gun that is never reported to the police, though it does prematurely spell the end of my time at Vinnie's. Indulging my firearms habit further, I buy a pistol for self-protection and get into the habit of sleeping with it next to me. One night I'm under the impression that my religious roommate is away, but at some point in the night there is a tap on my shoulder. I wake up and grab at the pistol, pointing it straight at the forehead of my assailant. My roommate screams in terror and rushes out into the corridor, before I realise what I've done.

Following this incident, I'm cast out of the St Vincent de Paul hostel and have to fend for myself. Fortunately for me, they don't get the police involved. Soon I fall in with a bunch of young blokes who I know from the streets outside Vinnie's. They are a motley crew – Brian, Robert, a tall skinny guy whose name I can never remember, and another bloke called Cain. We become regulars at a very rough pub nearby. We settle down in a corner each night with all the doors in sight and watch the glasses sailing past, wiping our feet on the way out.

I live in 13 places in Launceston in a single year. I work lots of crappy jobs – manual labour, meat factories, that sort of thing. I bust a gut – but I'm not sure why, because I'm not saving any money and I don't have any ambition. I don't have a girlfriend or even any good friends who care about me or want the best for me. Brian, Robert, Cain, and the other one are just drunks like me. I spend my time breaking and entering but get caught repeatedly, and the local police begin to grow tired of me. After every court appearance I make for burglary, I have to pay a fine, which I don't have enough money to pay without robbing somewhere else, and then I get caught and fined again. It goes on and on like that, in a never-ending circle. Breaking and entering used to be a childhood adventure – how far could I go, and what could I get away with? I did it to rebel and to gain independence from my abusers. It was just childish fun; there was no malice in it, and I never stole anything particularly valuable. But as an adult, I am stealing for survival. And eventually, they do send me down.

One Sunday I'm at the pub with a bunch of the boys and have the bright idea of breaking into one of the meat factories that I've been working in and taking as much beef as we can carry. It's just a stupid idea, and it never occurs to me that I could end up going to prison for it. I tell them how to get in and am given the job of being the lookout – the kookaburra, as we call it – while the others go in to loot the place. I sit in the car drinking cans of beer. The booze makes me woozy, and I start throwing the odd one into the road to keep myself awake, watching the beer spray out of it and spin around on the tarmac. But at some point, I doze off.

I wake up to a man in uniform tapping on the car window, and see my mates lined up in handcuffs against the factory wall.

It's a straightforward case – we've been caught in the act – and due to my previous offences, and the fact that I'm now an adult, I'm handed 10 months in prison. The other guys get 18 months, 16 months and 14 months because they are more seasoned criminals than me, but they rightly blame me for the whole thing, both because it was my idea in the first place and because I fell asleep when I was meant to be on the lookout. We're so amateurish and stupid that we become the laughing stock of the whole town – and if that isn't bad enough, I've lost my drinking buddies too.

We are sent to Risdon Prison in Hobart, which is widely known as "the pink palace", thanks to its colourful paintwork. I'm no more than a number now – prisoner 224/77, the 224th inmate of 1977. I go to see the governor soon after arriving, and we have a good chat. When he gets up to send me on my way, he says, "Well, you seem like a decent young man, Wilton, and it sounds like you've had a tough time of it. I think it's only fair for me to give you two months' remission." This means that I only have eight months to do inside. I get on with it, and the time goes by quite quickly.

Prison feels like just another institution, but the difference here is that we only have cold water and only one razor blade a week to shave with. The blades cut my face to ribbons. You are only allowed to grow a beard if you had one when you went in.

My cell is in the wing for first-timers, but I'm in there with a murderer. He is albino and people pick on him, which makes me nervous. The inside of our prison block is painted entirely yellow. There are probably 40 cells in the wing, divided between the two floors. There's a railing all the way around the first floor that looks down onto the ground floor. We're locked up at 8pm, and lights out is at 10pm. We aren't allowed any writing materials or books and have nothing to entertain ourselves with in the evening. You can talk to your next-door neighbour by shouting to him through the bars, but that's it. When I get up each morning, my top blanket has to be folded – it reminds me of the regime that I endured for years at Tresca. The blankets have to be arranged in a particular order, with the pillow on top. There's an unmovable fitted desk and a sink right by the window, with a stainless steel mirror so scratched that I can't see anything in it.

I have a job making water tanks, for fire trucks and farms. The other guys on the job are lifers. My task is to lie inside the tank and hold the rivets in place while they whack them in. At lunchtime, they tap the tank to let me know that I can come out. I have to admit that I respect the lifers. At least they are now doing something for the community – making water tanks for the fire trucks and for farms – and they don't grumble, they just get on with their jobs.

The rest of the people in prison are okay. I play a lot of cricket – against the guards and even against other prisons. It's through prison that I meet a bloke called Bruce. He's an unbelievably fast bowler, but he just can't get me out. I put absolutely everything in the way to stop him. He rants and raves at me, protesting, "Why didn't you hit the bloody thing?" And I simply reply, "It was going too fast!"

Of all the people in there, Bruce helps me the most. He takes me under his wing, showing me how things are done on the outside in the tank workshop – and I never have to get into one again. I start work outside the tank, bashing the rivets in while someone other poor sod goes inside to hold them in place. Bruce gives me a word of advice: "When you get out, go straight." He's in there for life, so he has nothing to lose.

We can write letters but they're censored, and we can read magazines but they're limited. So I keep to myself as much as I can. My friends who got sentenced with me have been to prison before. One of them works in the kitchen and is responsible for serving the food – which helps, as he gives me big portions, despite my failure in the robbery.

A rumour starts going round that I set up the robbery and that I should have got a longer sentence than the others. But I didn't organise it – it was just an off-the-cuff thing that we decided to do when we were drunk. I think they just resent the fact that I got a shorter sentence than them, because I'm younger and less ingrained with criminality.

Prison life in winter is horrible. Bleak. We can hear trains, so I imagine we're near a railway station. When I leave, I'll be given a travel ticket home, plus any money I've earned since coming here.

Seven months into my sentence, the governor calls me in.

"Son, I've got some news – I'm afraid your appeal has failed."

"What appeal?"

"The appeal that was lodged to clear you of the charges and take this off your criminal record."

I stare at him in confusion. I didn't know anything about any appeal and it feels unfair to be telling me about it just a month before I'm due to be released. I leave the governor's office in a confused rage, and walk back towards the cellblock.

On the way back I hear footsteps and sense another inmate following me. Suddenly the steps speed up, and panic rises in my stomach. I wheel around before he can get his hands on me and grab him by the collar, slamming him into the wall.

"If you do that again," I shout in his face, "I'll kill you."

He looks stunned and dazed, but I instantly realise that he wasn't following me at all. My traumatic experience four years ago has made me paranoid about being attacked again, and I acted instinctively in self-defence. A guard's hand clamps around my arm and hauls me off him. I'm too ashamed to explain what made me do it, and the governor is furious with me. I lose my two months' remission.

I would have been out in a few weeks, but I end up confined for another two months. I try to shrug it off and get on with my sentence, but something triggered that anger. Something that the governor could never understand.

11.

WILTON NO MORE

Thankfully, the last two months of my sentence fly by. When they tell me I'll be going home tomorrow, I make my bed in the evening and sit on it all night, waiting for dawn. I get up the following morning and they take me back into the guard room and give me back what little I brought with me.

I'm released with a ticket for the journey home and $17 in wages from the work I've been doing on the water tanks. But there's a pub down the road from the prison, where a drink costs 30 cents. What else can I do? I head straight in, get pissed and miss my train home. Getting a later train home means I miss my appointment with my probation officer, who I am supposed to see that afternoon.

It's not the best way to start my life outside prison and, even after all those months of reflection, I basically carry on where I left off, especially with alcohol. Before long I'm getting arrested again for various drunken misdemeanours. I can't see that I have an alcohol problem at this point – I feel like I'm just a young guy going out and trying to integrate into society. The hardest part of being an ex-crim is getting a job, with no references and no qualifications. The only real experience I have is doing metalwork in prison, but it's hard to tell potential employers that the only work experience you have is from prison!

I even try to join the merchant navy: I meet up with an old friend who has a big pirate earring, but the guy due to interview us takes one look at us and says, "I'm not hiring no fucking queers." I think it's my friend's earring he objects to, but I would have been too frightened to go and interview alone, because I don't have the courage to do things for myself.

My instinctive reaction to difficult situations is violence, and it isn't always drink-related: sometimes if I don't like a guy, I'll just panic and give him a smack. I see what I presume is a threat and strike first, even if it turns out they only wanted to pat me on the back. I do have some rules, though. I never get in bar fights, for instance – I only go to bars to have a drink and always try

ABOVE: My grandfather, my uncle Arthur Wade, and my mother. BELOW LEFT: My mother, Marina Violet Wade. This is one of very few photos I have of her. BELOW RIGHT: My father, Ronald Wilton.

ABOVE: Kevin and me during the early years in Cornwall. I was given these photos from our childhood much later on in my life. BELOW LEFT: Kevin and me shortly before leaving Rose Cottage. BELOW RIGHT: Me mucking about outside Rose Cottage.

ABOVE: Rose Cottage: the beautiful house where we grew up, situated at the heart of Heligan Woods in Mevagissey, Cornwall. BELOW: L to R – Bruce, me, Kevin, Pete, Margaret and Caroline.

ABOVE: Kevin, Bruce and me. BELOW LEFT: My original passport photo for the journey to Australia. BELOW RIGHT: Me in my Exeter District School uniform. You can see my chipped front tooth from the wheelbarrow incident with Harry.

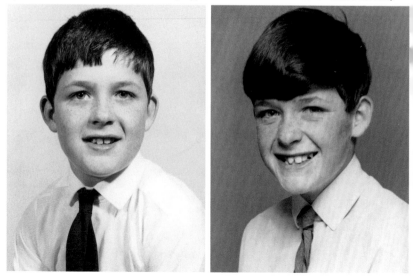

ABOVE: Harry and Lily Richmond, who took charge of us at Tresca.
LEFT: Me with Shep, the family dog when I was married to Helen in Tasmania.
BELOW: Kevin and me in 1983.

ABOVE: My late second wife Christine, her son Harry, and me. BELOW: Receiving one of my awards for excellent service at the hotel in Moretonhampstead – the first time I felt I had taken real pride in my work.

ABOVE: Me and Annie ready to go on our first date. BELOW: Our wedding on 3 July 2007 – the happiest day of my life.

ABOVE: Celebrating good times on the Bude Canal with my Annie.

to respect the owners. My fights always happen outside – if someone pisses me off inside, I'll wait until we're outside to have a fight. I'm lucky to come out of some of the scrapes I get into. Sometimes I've had to run as fast as hell and just hope that the other guy isn't as quick.

One night I go to a funny old place called the Launceston Hotel. There's a long bar and at one end is an ashtray at an angle so that when you run water though it, you get rid of all the butts in one go. I go there with a friend, and we're already half cut. We get to the bar, sit down on a stool, and order a drink. He asks me where the toilet is and spins round. He thinks he's already got there, when all he's actually done is spin around on his stool. Then, without realising where he is, he starts pissing in the cigarette tray. I can't believe my eyes, but am too concerned about drawing attention to ourselves to alert anyone or have a go at him. When he finishes, propped up at the bar, he finds that his elbow is jammed between the bar and the armrest, and he can't get it out. We both yank at his arm for a good half hour, but eventually have to call the fire brigade to get him out. I'm so unimpressed with him that I leave him there while he waits for them to arrive. He is furious that I've abandoned him, but I don't care – I might have a bad record of my own, but I never treat other people's property with such disrespect.

Another time I go to a nightclub and sit in a corner, quietly drinking a jug of beer. That night there's a raid by the police licensing squad to check if everyone there is of age. I've just turned 19, and when I look up, there's a man in uniform asking me if I'm 18. I'm not 18 anymore and tell him so — so he drags me outside and kicks the shit out of me, before telling me to piss off and stop being such a cheeky bastard. I don't understand what I did wrong — after all, they didn't ask my age! This gives me yet more reason to hate the police, and I start sneaking up to parked police cars and let down their tyres. I stick my fingers up at them when I see them around. They are corrupt and aggressive and I hate their guts.

My alcohol problem gets out of control and I become dependent on it to the point that I can't hold a job down. I even go back to St Vincent de Paul's to rob the place, because I know there's a safe in the corner of the foyer. I know where the bolt goes across and how to get through it. With the help of a friend, I put a jemmy bar under the bolt and whack it repeatedly with a hammer. Half an hour later, the safe opens, and there are bags and bags of coins. We put them in a car and drive up the road to a place called Invermay, on the outskirts of Launceston. We bury our treasure next to a concrete slab in a paddock, but when we go back a week later, they've put a bridge stanchion over the top of it, so we can't get to it. My friend accuses me of stealing it from him, and we end up punching each other.

At this point, my brain is totally fogged with alcohol. Something is deeply wrong with me – I can't even deal with the proceeds of my crimes properly. And that has become the story of my life. It really sinks in, chewing at me all the time. I hate my past and my present, and I can't see any future at all. It gets even worse when I'm on the booze. When I've had a drink, if I'm not turning my violent streak on other people, I turn it on myself. I take a razor blade out and start slashing deep crimson welts into my arms and my face. I burn my skin with red-hot pokers. If I feel under my beard, I can feel the indentations from where I put the poker. I hate what I stand for, and what I'm doing with my life. I feel like I've never been accepted by anyone – I have been disowned.

There are gaps between my periods of self-harm, but subconsciously I am doing it constantly. I don't like who I am, and I think that if I make myself look ugly I won't have to deal with anybody else. And that's why I cut my own face. I am terrified of people seeing the scars, so I wear long-sleeved shirts and I don't go out until the scars have healed up. Scars and burns and cuts don't heal in a week, so I stay at home for days and refuse to answer the door. Sometimes I even run out of food and drink, and still I refuse to go outside. I make coffee using hot water from the tap instead of boiling it, even though it makes me ill. And somehow I feel that I deserve it.

I couldn't tell you how I celebrated my eighteenth birthday, or my twenty-first. By the start of the 1980s, I've completely lost touch with Kevin. The Richmonds don't tell me where he has gone, but I bump into one of the psychologists from the Department of Social Security called Tony and he tells me that Kevin is somewhere on the mainland. However, he warns me Kevin might not want to see me, and says he needs to check with him before he puts us in touch. I want to see my brother again, so I resolve to head to the mainland and find him.

Soon after that I do a breaking and entering job that I'm sure I'll get caught for, so I decide to kill two birds with one stone and escape to the mainland, so I can see Kevin while I'm at it. I have virtually no money, but I get in touch with Tony and he says it isn't a problem – he'll pay my fare over to Melbourne on the condition that I do something for him.

Tony asks me to come and stay at his house before I leave for the mainland, and I agree. The day I arrive, he says he has to go out and that while he's gone, I must catalogue all of his books in alphabetical order, to pay him back for my fare. I spend the whole day doing it, and when he comes back he says, "I've got a surprise for you tomorrow." In the morning, he accompanies me across the Bass Strait and drives me to a military base, where I'm reunited with Kevin.

I haven't seen Kevin for two years. He has joined the navy. He thinks I abandoned him, but I think he abandoned me – Harry and Lily put him in the navy to keep him away from me. It's a strange meeting – someone takes a photo of us and in it we're standing there, unsmiling, like two thugs. I blame myself for the strain between us, because I got Kevin into trouble – after all, he did once appear in court because of me – and I should have been the responsible older brother. We have a few drinks and talk about general things, but not about our feelings. It's over almost as soon as it has begun.

I cannot go straight back to Tasmania, because I'm on the run. From Melbourne I hitchhike the thousands of miles to Rockhampton in Queensland in a kind of alcoholic haze. I find a hostel there and it is boiling hot. Someone shows me to a camp bed with a couple of blankets on it and I fall asleep on it. The next thing I know, I am semi-delirious and being taken to Rockhampton Hospital.

I am severely dehydrated and spend the next four days there. The attendants push me in a wheelchair out onto the first-floor veranda, where I sit for hours at a time, thinking about how I can possibly turn my life around.

When I'm discharged from the hospital at Rockhampton, I plan to go all the way to Coober Peddy in the centre of Australia. On the way there I go to a bar with fantastically cold air conditioning, where I have a couple of drinks and fall asleep in the garden. The next day I hitch a lift as far as Tenant Creek, where I spend days stealing wallets in bars until I have enough to buy a car, an old jalopy that costs me $100 and that is not taxed or insured. I drive down the longest, straightest road you can imagine. In the far distance I catch sight of a tiny blue square; as it gets bigger, I realise it is a sign, and eventually the text is legible: "No petrol for 700 miles." I only have a tankful, so I go all the way back to Rockhampton to get some jerry cans and fill them up.

After a long and gruelling drive, I eventually get to Coober Peddy. It's an amazing place, where lots of people live in underground caves to keep them cool. It's fascinating to find windows and front doors in the middle of the rocks. I walk through one of them and find myself in a museum, which is a surreal experience.

I head back towards Tenant Creek and try to find more legitimate ways of making money along the way. I see some amazing things – like twelve-feet-tall termite mounds. I work as a grape picker for about a week, and somewhere between Tennant Creek and Brisbane I get a job fertilising. They have just clear-felled an entire hillside of trees, and I and twenty other people have to a carry around a little cup and a sack of fertiliser and spread the fertiliser around the stumps, so that the rain will wash it down into the tree roots. At the end of the day, they serve a huge meal in a work shack at the bottom of the hill. I also pick watermelons and work in a timber yard for a while.

I don't travel in any structured way – I don't plan a route or even really know where I am on a map. I end up going to the Gold Coast, which is bloody horrible. There are huge high-rises on the beach, and as I drive along, all I can see is endless people streaming out of them towards the seaside. The sounds, the sights, the heat… I can't stand any of it. I just want to keep going. Eventually I make my way back to Melbourne, and I have enough money for a flight back to Tasmania. I'm glad that I have been to the mainland, though – it was a real eye-opener.

At some point soon after that I go to see the Richmonds. Kevin stays with them when he's back from leave, and I go to see him, but afterwards I wish I hadn't. The children's home closed down soon after I left – we were the last children to be shipped over from London – and they have bought the house just off the main road, close to Tresca. I'm glad that they don't have the chance to make any more neglected children suffer, but it infuriates me to think that if Margaret had kept us for just another few months, we might never have been sent away to live with them.

It was a mistake to go and see them. I could have killed them for what they did to me. Harry says that he did everything he could to make me into a nice person, and he is sorry that he failed. I tell him he has ruined my life and that I hope I'll never see them again.

I get a phone call from the Tasmanian social services soon afterwards, and they tell me, "We have an inheritance for you." They ask me to come in and collect it and sign for it. They don't give me any more information than that – I don't know who it's from, when they died or why they have left me money.

I go to collect it, but when I sign the paper they hand over the tiny sum of $5. I am absolutely baffled – first that someone should bequeath me such a tiny amount, and second that nobody would tell me who it was from. I suddenly realise that I really want to find out more about my family and reconnect with them – I'm convinced that there's more to this inheritance than meets the eye. I've always wanted to find out what happened after my mum put us up for fostering, but I now realise that this information isn't just going to present itself to me on a plate.

I start hunting for more information and begin to write letters – to social services in Tasmania and the Fairbridge Society in London, who were responsible for sending us here. Their reply says that they can't give me any information because it would be detrimental to my health, so I break in to the social services department in Launceston to try and find out for myself. I manage to find a few documents providing an overview of my case, but not much detail. The only thing that rings a bell is the name of the lady from Cornwall Social Services – Dorothy Watkins. I commit the name to memory. Unfortunately, I get done for breaking in to the building – it is pretty obvious who has done it, as I make no attempt to cover my tracks – and I'm fined again.

At this point, I decide not to use my father's name anymore. As long as I've been a Wilton, I've never really liked it and I've tried to use it only when I have to. The name always reminds me of Wilton Carpets, which then reminds me of how long I've spent being walked over by everybody – Pete, Harry, school bullies and teachers have already wiped their feet on me and I'm determined that I'm not going to be anyone's carpet again. That was what it was like from the moment I found out I was adopted up until my deportation to Australia. I decide to make a change and take my mother's name, Wade.

I also start to use various other names. I feel like I've lost a grasp of my own identity, and so I like to remain anonymous. I travel around Tasmania using the name Gideon Tanner, which I stole from a Kenny Rogers song. Another one I use is Xer Edaw, which is my name backwards. I stay at the Cradle Mountain reserve in Tasmania and go in as Gideon Tanner, but by the time I come out I'm Xer Edaw. As I travel around, I variously introduce myself to people as Gideon Tanner, Rex Wade and Xer Edaw; I never meet those people again, but I sometimes wonder which name they'll remember me by.

12.

FAMILY

I realise that in order to find out more about myself I'll need to come back to the UK – that's where most of the answers are, and it's also where I'll have the best chance of finding out about my mum.

Around the time I realise this, I'm working in a factory that makes metal moulds. There are a number of ex-cons like me on their books. We go to the pub in the evenings and have a good laugh – and I'm a little sad at the thought that I might have to leave them all behind once I've saved up enough money.

But then one evening I meet a lady called Helen, who changes everything. She's standing on the other side of the pub with some friends and I catch her eye across a sea of faces. Up until this point I've never been in a relationship with a woman – I've been too busy being confined at home, drunk on the streets or in prison. In many ways, while I know I have issues, on another level I'm having the time of my life living as I am. However, I decide to take the risk, and when I go over and talk to her she is friendly and warm. We arrange to have coffee the next day at a Christian coffee shop.

And it goes well. I make up some stories about my past and avoid telling her about my drinking and my time in prison, because I'm ashamed – I keep those stories hidden away, because I'm desperate not to lose her straight away. One of the *Jaws* films has just been released, so we go to see it at the cinema in town, before heading up to the Cataract Gorge on the edge of Launceston – a really beautiful, deep wooded area, with the South Esk River running through it into deep natural basins that are like small lakes. There's also an outdoor swimming pool, cafés, a suspension bridge and a chairlift. Around the swimming pool there's a grassy area where people have picnics, so we sit down with a few beers and she gets into her swimming costume and jumps into the pool.

"Shark!" I yell, and you've never seen a girl get out of the water so quickly – along with everyone else in the pool! That evening we kiss for the first time and it's strange and wonderful and unlike anything I've ever felt.

We go out for a good while, and I realise what a lovely lady she is: funny, witty, pretty, with a charming shaggy-dog hairstyle. I even get on well with her brother Ranga (who gained this nickname because of his orange hair and long arms, which make him look a bit like an orangutan).

Eventually I ask Helen to marry me. She says yes, and I'm over the moon. The wedding is just a tiny ceremony at the registry office, nothing grand. She soon gets pregnant and we move into a newly built single-storey house in the suburb of Newnham, in one of the estates that are springing up all over Launceston. They haven't finished the estate yet, and our bungalow is next to an enormous paddock. The house is lovely and the plot is massive. We get a dog called Shep and then our beautiful son Joshua is born. All this makes me begin to believe that I might finally have a happy future. The three of us have a good life.

At this point I'm doing proper jobs, things like woodcutting and forestry. I have a truck licence, which means I can also get work as a delivery driver. This job involves delivering gelignite in one truck and detonator cord in a separate one (it wouldn't be the best idea for both things to be in the same truck!) and it pays good money. I also take a job for a company called Charlie Fluff, driving all over Tasmania to fill people's roofs with insulation made out of recycled paper and with borax. I turn up at people's houses and pump the material into their roof space through a big tube. On several occasions the pipe accidentally goes through the ceiling, and their house ends up full of Charlie Fluff!

I frequently spend many hours on the road with work, and by the time I get home, all I want is to go for a drink with my mates at the pub. I sometimes drive home drunk, hoping that I won't get caught – that's how it becomes clear to me that a happy and normal life is still out of my reach. I start to get drunk every day and have furious rows with Helen, who doesn't think I'm in a fit state to look after our child. I fight my corner as best as I can, but eventually have to concede that she's right. I'm still a drinker, and I feel guilty and ashamed that I didn't tell her about my problems at the start of our relationship. I start to believe that our marriage has always been a lie, because it was founded on false images of who I really was. It is my first relationship and I got swept up, without knowing what I was doing. I decide that I have to move out.

As my marriage falls apart, my defence mechanism kicks in, and I become aggressive and angry about the fact that I've lost my wife and son. Kevin despises me, too – when I see him again, he confronts me over the fact that I didn't go to his wedding. I tell him that I couldn't go because I wasn't in touch with him, and the Richmonds hadn't told me he was getting married. I would have given everything to go to his wedding had I known about it, and the Richmonds could have told me about it – but they didn't.

I move into a grotty flat on my own, and visit Helen and Joshua when I can. I try to visit only when I'm sober, but one weekend when Josh is about three years old, I've been drinking before going to see him. Helen says she has to go out for a minute and we start arguing, because I think she's trying to avoid me. As soon as she's left, I begin to smash everything up in the hallway, kicking the place to pieces.

Joshua is standing in the middle of the lounge and bawling. I know that I've made him cry and I'm scaring him, and I hate myself for what I have become. The din he's making brings home just how unfit a father I am. And then I do something that I'll regret for the rest of my life. I whack him around the head and as he falls to the floor, I yell at him to stand up again. And then, as he does, I kick his legs out from underneath him.

It's only then that I realise what I've done, and it hits me like a train. Helen appears and jumps on me, wrestling me to the ground. She screams at me to get out of the house and never come back. I despise myself.

I've struck a defenceless child. There never has been, and never will be, any excuse for my behaviour and at that moment I realise I am doing to my own son exactly what Pete and Harry did to me.

Helen has no choice but to bring the police into it and I end up in court, charged with battery to a minor. This time, I'm not the victim of violence – I'm the perpetrator. As well as excruciating sadness and shame about what I did to my son, another fear is that I will have to go back to prison – and if I do go back, as a reoffender, I could be sentenced to a lot longer this time. I am charged and bailed and it will be another few months before the case comes back to court.

I realise that I need to change. I concede that I'm an alcoholic and understand that I need to stop drinking. I've been to clinics before, but every time I've come out I've gone for a drink right away, because the drinking is a crutch. Not all of the disappointment I've experienced could have been prevented, but I haven't done anything constructive about it – I've just relied on alcohol.

I try really hard to sober up and get the most responsible job I'd ever had – as a foreman, helping to install irrigation systems in sports grounds. I live in an apartment and with my court appearance approaching, Helen calls me to chat. She seems surprisingly friendly, which I can't understand

– surely she should be angry with me for what I did, but I sense that she's trying to include me as the father of our child. I think she sees that I'm trying to change.

Fearing prison, I make a momentous decision, but keep it secret from everyone. I sell everything I own – my white Chrysler Valiant and virtually all my belongings – and buy a plane ticket to England. The night before I leave, Helen turns up at my flat, and she brings Josh with her. We have a friendly conversation, but I can't stop thinking that I'm lying to her, because I can't tell her that I'm leaving the following morning. I say goodbye to them both and give Josh a hug and a kiss. Neither of them know it, but they won't see me again for many years. At 7am the next morning I head to Launceston Airport and from there I fly to Melbourne, to Hong Kong, and on to London.

I've never forgiven myself for running off like that, because it repeated a pattern from my own life for my son. I'd been an abandoned child myself, and I set it off again in Josh – I just hoped that he wouldn't go the way that I had. It's no good me hiding from the truth – I want to tell the reality of what's happened to me, even if it doesn't make me look good. Looking back on my life, hurting Joshua is the thing that upsets me the most, and so it's a memory that I've tried to keep tucked away. It was fundamentally wrong of me to abandon him, and it has affected me as well as him. Now, when I see a child fall over in the street, I don't go anywhere near them – I have a fear of picking up children, because all I can see is Josh and what I did to him. I brought a wonderful human into the world – and then I hurt him. I have had to live with what I did – knowing not only that I hit my son, but that I abandoned him, leaving him and his mother to fend for themselves.

PART III

RETURN

13.

ANSWERS

At the heart of my story is a mystery, and the mystery is my mother. There's very little I know about her, and that fact haunts me every day of my life. Her name was Marina Violet Wade and she was born in 1936. She married my father and became Marina Violet Wilton. After leaving my father, she married for a second time and became Marina Violet Ware. The fact that she had three surnames, all beginning with W, has added to the difficulty in trying to trace what happened to her. She was sighted at my grandmother's funeral in 1966, but she did not attend her father's funeral in 1975.

Beyond those few facts, there's almost nothing I can say about her. I can't remember anything about her, not her scent, nor her face. I am a motherless child, so in that sense I am also an orphan, because although my mother disappeared, the fate of my father is much more certain: he died from a burst appendix in Redruth in Cornwall in 1962, in the same hospital where I was born.

My mother is a stranger to me who is illuminated by neither stories, anecdotes nor rumours. She vanished into thin air as though she was a phantom who arrived in this world only to give birth to me and my brothers, before leaving again.

It was 1986. I had returned to England for the first time in 16 years – and it felt strange. Having been regarded as a Pom in Tasmania, I now felt more of an Australian than an Englishman, though the truth is that I was actually neither – I was stuck between the two, and didn't really feel a part of either country. My accent was either Cornish with an Australian twang, or Australian with a Cornish burr – in fact, it still is. I suppose that I was both Australian and English, but I just felt displaced. I felt I had been treated badly by both Britain and Australia.

I caught the train from London to Plymouth, looking out at the unfamiliar landscape – the hedgerows and the pylons, the road signs and the old stone buildings, the Somerset Levels and the Quantock Hills, the seafront at Dawlish, the rolling hills and steep valleys. It all seemed new, and yet I could feel some familiarity with it, in the recesses of my memory.

Before leaving Tasmania I'd written a letter to my Uncle Alan and Auntie Yvonne who lived in Torpoint, just across the water from Plymouth. They said that I could come and stay with them, and met me at the station. The first thing Alan said to me was not, "Hello, how are you?" but, "Boy, you look like your mother." And I said the first thing that came into my head in response, which was, "My mother never had a beard." I didn't know what else to say! We went back to their house, where Yvonne had made a meal.

We started talking about my mother but when I asked questions about her, they just said, "That was a long time ago – it's in the past." It was like that for a week – they'd talk about my dad, but never mentioned details about my mother. On my birth certificate it reveals that my dad, Ronald Garfield Wilton, was a commercial traveller when I was born, and lived with my mother in Lanivet, a small village not far from Bodmin. But there's no information at all about my mother.

I couldn't get to the bottom of the mystery, even though I found out that when I was at the children's home in Newquay, my parents had lived just four miles away. No one at Cornwall Social Services had made any attempt to contact any of my family about taking us in – Alan and Yvonne said that they would have gladly looked after us, but they weren't asked.

Before I left, I asked if they could show me some family photos. They presented me with a couple, but the strange and unsettling thing was that they had cut my mother out of each one. Even in their wedding photo they had cut a straight line between my mum and dad, leaving just my father in the picture. Can you imagine – a wedding photo of a groom without a bride! In another one they had literally cut out my mother's face, and gave me the remainder of the photograph. When I asked them why they had done it, they merely said, "It's all a long time ago now," as though that was a sufficient answer. They gave me some photos of my dad, but they'd cut my mother out of those ones, too. Whatever it was that my mother did, I don't give a damn – she's still my mother, and if she hurt that side of the family, that's their problem and not mine.

The only possible reason I can think of is that she did something to bring shame to the family; I can't see any other reason why she'd have been shunned like that. I've been led to believe that she was suffering from post-natal depression when Kevin and I were born, but that's just conjecture. I think that maybe she had a mental health problem. She wouldn't have been able to get any help from the state at that time and would have had to choose between working and looking after us children. If she was seen to have brought shame on the family, then I can only guess that it was something to do with her mental health or a sexual or moral indiscretion. Did she get put inside a mental hospital, or did she work as a prostitute? Those were the main taboos at the time, and I have no idea which of these possible explanations is most plausible – it's all total speculation.

My aunt and uncle were certainly not forthcoming and as I'd come to see them specifically to find out information, I felt badly hurt. I don't think you should blame a child for their parents' actions, but it felt as if they had disowned me. I had no idea what the secret was – and it didn't matter to me anyway, because I didn't care what she had done. I just wanted to know the truth about what happened to her.

I was sure that someone, somewhere, knew whether my mother was alive or dead. And I wished they would let *me* know. That was all I wanted. It had gone on for too long. If she was dead, then I needed to know – I didn't want to have to carry on speculating.

After leaving Torpoint, I bought a bike and cycled from Plymouth back to Heligan Woods, near Rose Cottage. I stayed there for about a week, rough camping – all I had with me was my bike and a couple of panniers of stuff. I hadn't known where else to go, so I went to the place that felt most like home. But Margaret wasn't there, and nor were Bruce or Kevin – it was just me, alone, in the woods. I went into Mevagissey, where I met people who had known me as a child. The strangest thing was that I had no recollection of them, but they remembered me, and bought me drinks. There were people who knew me when I was a child, including some who had taken us in at one point when we ran away from Pete. I went to the same bar every night, because I got to hear stories about all the things that I got up to and all the trouble I made when I was a child. It was great fun, and I was happy to be back near the only home I'd ever known, but I didn't have any place to wash apart from the creek in the woods and I was getting dirty. I sold my pushbike, and pretty quickly ran out of money and needed a job. I didn't know there was something called the job centre in England – I'd been looking for the "labour exchange", and when I asked someone, they told me I needed to go to the job centre in St Austell. I eventually applied for a position working with the Youth Training Scheme as a maintenance worker, doing all kinds of odd jobs. I worked there for just over nine months – the money wasn't too bad and enabled me to get me back on my feet financially. I found accommodation in a caravan site on the coast near St Austell at a place called Duporth, just five or six miles away from Mevagissey. It was a small site with six vans, and I was given the crumby one on the end. It wasn't warm, but it was my own place, and right next door there was a holiday camp with a bar, so I could go there and pretend I was a camper on the site.

The job was brilliant, because it gave me enough money to live on, as well as a base from which I could meet a lot of people from my past. I even went to hunt down the school bully Ant Miller, just to see what he looked like. I'd heard that he still lived in the area and was a regular at Kelly's Milk Bar in Mevagissey, where I used to go as a kid. It hadn't changed much. I sat down and said to a girl working there, "Do you know a bloke called Ant Miller?" And she said, "Yeah, he'll be here in a minute." But when I saw him, I didn't have the heart to confront him, though I couldn't forgive him for how he had treated me.

I was desperate to find out more about what had happened to me. I still had the piece of paper that I had stolen from the social services office in Launceston, and tried to track down Dorothy Watkins, the head of the department in Cornwall, who I believed was the person who instigated it all. It was like trying to find a needle in a haystack, but in 1987 or 1988 I found out where she lived. She was called

Mrs Fox by then, and lived near Truro. I went to her house, knocked on her door and when she answered I explained who I was. And as I looked at her, I recognised the woman who I had first seen at Rose Cottage all those years ago.

I was not aggressive, and she seemed quite pleased to see me and invited me into her house for a cup of tea. But then she said it: "What I did was for the best for all of you."

Well, by now, you'll know that quite frankly, I think that's a load of crap. I'd been separated from my family, split up from my brother and sent thousands of miles away to live in a brutal children's home, and it was all "for the best"? I was shocked, but she honestly seemed to think that sending us away should have given us a better life. She seemed a very gentle and sincere woman, but she hadn't told us the truth. She had come to Rose Cottage and sold us the idea of going to Australia as part of the Fairbridge scheme, telling us "we do not split families". She convinced us that we'd have a better life, but all along Bruce was out of the picture, and although she may have believed that the Fairbridge scheme would be good for us, we soon came to know the reality. Cornwall Social Services had clearly decided what was going to happen to us – we were suddenly put in the children's home in August and left the country in December. But what was their incentive to get us there so quickly, and why did they split us up from Bruce? He may already have felt separate from us, but that was because of all the disruption with Pete – any responsible childcare service should have done their best to keep us together, not to tear us apart. I don't think the people at Fairbridge understood what was going on in their overseas homes – they can't have known about all the cruelty and nastiness. But they owned the homes and ran the scheme, so they should have known and done something about it.

I've got a copy of Dorothy Watkins' autobiography. It's called *Other People's Children – Adventures in Childcare* and she clearly states in it that she believed all the way to the end of the Fairbridge scheme that sending kids like Kevin and me to Australia was a good thing. When I spoke to the Child Migrants Trust, they told me that she was an extremely difficult case and wasn't able to see the pain and the devastation that those decisions had caused.

Although I had tried to steer clear of alcohol in my final months in Tasmania, I was drinking with a passion when I arrived back in Cornwall. At first, when I lived in Heligan Woods, I would travel into Mevagissey to drink in the pubs and all kinds of people would buy me drinks. And then, when I got a job, I would drink at the holiday resort and in the pubs in Mevagissey. I realised that I was falling back into an alcoholic haze. I bought myself a little moped and one evening I went down to the village and started drinking. I was in a pub when I suddenly saw my old nemesis Tim Bale, Ant Miller's old sidekick, just sitting there – and was so angry with him for what he'd done to me as a child that I went up to him and gave him a complete mouthful. As I left the pub, I heard a woman say, "And don't you ever come back, you bastard." I can't remember what the pub was called, but I never did go back there again. I got on my moped and started up the hill towards Pentewan. I hadn't noticed that they were doing some roadworks there, and I went straight into them and crashed to the floor. My helmet flew off and I just lay on the ground, laughing my head off. I somehow managed to get home, and it was only the next day that I realised how battered and bruised I was.

Soon after that, I moved to a new place in St Austell, a sort of hotel that had been converted. It was there that I met two Canadian Mormon missionaries. I've got nothing against religion – it's only when it's rammed down my throat that I retaliate – and these two were absolutely fantastic. I got on with them really well. They came down into the communal kitchen and asked my name; in mock formality, I said, "Wade, Rex" – so from then on they called me Wade. I got them talking, and asked them to sit down have a drink with me. They said no, but I insisted and got them steaming drunk. They were great fun. Things like that always went on – I'd meet people and get on with them but then never see them again. I've always been useless at keeping up friendships, because I've been so unreliable. Lots of people have given up on me, and I don't blame them for it.

If I try to think about who I actually met during that time, I can't really remember – it was just a drunken blur. I got so angry in the months following my encounter with Dorothy Watkins that I used to do idiotic things like rugby tackle plastic road signs and head-butt wine bottles to see if I could break them. I don't know if there was something about the mentality of that era that made these things seem acceptable – because there was a lot of rage around with punks and football hooligans and riots – but I think I was on a self-destructive mission. It got to the stage where I realised that I had a serious problem. I'd got in trouble with the law again, for the same sort of things that I'd done in Australia – breaking and entering and being drunk and disorderly. I always received fines instead of being sent to prison, but I was eventually put on probation and was sent for counselling for alcohol abuse. I got through the counselling, but didn't approach it in a very honest way, because I wanted to carry on drinking.

I'd always drink Scotch before I went to the pub and always thought that if I could count how many drinks I'd had, then I wasn't really drunk. When I went out I'd usually drink half a bottle of Scotch at home, and then I'd be well on the way. Then I'd go to the pub and have another drink, and another, and another. Nine times out of ten I never got home – I'd wake up in a hedge or in someone's shed, or I'd crash on someone's floor and wake up underneath the table. All I did was go out, night after night after night. It was a continual party, but there were times when I was between jobs that I was literally taking money from my electric meter to buy my next drink. It got to the stage where I was always searching for the next drink. It caused a lot of problems – financially, physically and mentally. I kept on having grey-outs and not being able to remember what had happened to me the previous day.

A couple of years after my return from Australia, I went to find Margaret, who'd moved away from Cornwall. I'd found out her details from Brenda, the woman who used to live at Heligan Mill, after I met her at a party in Mevagissey. They had stayed in touch, and she gave me Margaret's number. We arranged to meet at Paddington Station in London.

"But how will I recognise you?" she asked me.

"I'll be wearing a Fosters t-shirt," I replied.

She hadn't expected to see me an adult, because she remembered me as a child. The last time she had seen me

I'd been 11, but now I was 27. It was wonderful — she was still lovely, and she took me out for an Indian meal. Pete was there too — they were still together, but I was taller than him now. I didn't really want to talk to him, but was polite enough to say hello and shake his hand — though he still had the same menacing sneer whenever he spoke. But it was wonderful to see Margaret, who said, "I can still picture when you were 11, and look at you now." If I hadn't told her what I was wearing I doubt she would have recognised me, though I certainly would have recognised her.

We talked about the old times at Rose Cottage, and I asked about her daughter Caroline. She told me about Caroline's brother Daniel, who had arrived after Kevin and I had left for Australia. It was lovely, but after the meal that was it — I got back on the train again and went home.

I had a number of jobs at that time. At one point I worked for a wealthy bloke as a handyman at his house, in exchange for accommodation. Then I stacked shelves at a DIY store. I also spent a while travelling around England, installing hydraulic loading bays for a Dutch company. There was a gang of us who'd do the job together, staying in B&Bs and getting drunk together. It was fun, but I didn't feel like my life was going anywhere — in fact, it felt like it was going backwards.

When I had first arrived back in England, it felt as if I was on the run. I wasn't just trying to find out about my distant past – I was also running away from my more recent criminal past and the court case in Tasmania. I was using the name Rex Wade, partly because I was worried that the Australian authorities might be looking for me under the name of Rex Wilton, my legal name in Tasmania.

In the end I decided to go back to Tasmania, because my attempt to find out about my past wasn't getting anywhere: members of my family had died, those that were still alive were not answering my questions, and I was getting nothing from the authorities, despite all the letters I'd sent to them. It was no surprise to me that the authorities tried to prevent me from trying to find about the truth of my own history, but it was much more disturbing to realise that members of my own family were trying to do the same. No matter who I asked, I could never get any answers.

I had further trouble with the English authorities, because I didn't even have a National Insurance number and didn't know how to get one. When I tried to find out what I needed to do, they simply said, "Everyone has a National Insurance number. What's yours?" I explained that I had grown up in Tasmania, but they were not listening – they told me that even if I had grown up abroad, a number would have been sent to me. I was starting to get really fed up with life in the UK, and whenever I came into contact with the authorities, they didn't seem to take the time to listen.

One particular incident felt like the final straw. A friend of mine from Heligan Woods was concerned for my wellbeing and invited me round for dinner. He asked me how I was and listened to my stories of frustration, before telling me that a good meal would make me feel better. So he cooked me a mushroom omelette.

"Aren't you having any?" I asked, slightly confused when he gave me the whole thing.

"No, mate, it's all for you," he winked. "We need to sort you out before anything else, don't worry about me."

I was perplexed but touched by the gesture. After eating, I left his house and headed into Mevagissey. As I walked, I began to hear a monotonous and rhythmic booming noise. I thought I must have a headache coming on, but the noise of the blood pumping through my head got worse and worse. I went into a bar where they were playing music, and it drove me mad – this was the last thing I needed.

When I saw my friend a month later, he gave me a wry smile.

"How was the omelette?"

"What the hell was in it?" I asked him.

When he told me about the mushrooms he'd used in it, I flew off the handle. I didn't speak to him again for 14 years. I didn't care if he was trying to be helpful or trying to relax me – he had done the opposite, making me more anxious and paranoid than I'd ever been.

Before I left Cornwall, I went to a police station in Truro to find out whether I was wanted in Australia in connection with a crime. They couldn't find anything on their system, which meant that either the case had been dropped by the police or Helen had asked them not to pursue the charges against me.

14.

RETURN DOWN UNDER

I went back to Tasmania in March 1992. A ticket to Australia was very expensive in those days – much more so than it is now. I think it cost about £1,200. I'd already sold almost everything that I owned in order to try and finance the trip, including my white minivan that I had bought for £500. I took everything else I owned to a car boot sale in St Austell and got another hundred pounds, but I was still short.

Because I'd got into a few scrapes with the law, I'd been referred to a treatment centre at St Lawrence's Hospital in Bodmin. I went to the doctor to get medication to help with my alcohol addiction and ended up in a homeless shelter because I didn't have anywhere else to live. From there I was sent to Rashleigh House, a rehabilitation centre in St Lawrence's, for a few months. Part of my therapy there was to draw my life story in cartoon form. We also did group therapy, which I really hated. There was an old guy called Clifford, who always tried to wind other people up during the sessions – when it was his turn to speak, instead of saying something about himself, he used to fire a question at someone else. One day he asked me, "What is it that you really, really want?"

I said, "I really want to go to Oz."

"Well, how are you going to get there?" he asked.

I said I'd raised half of the money but I didn't know how I would get the rest. I didn't think anything would come of it, but Clifford was about to give me a big surprise: in another group meeting a couple of days later, he said he would pay for half my fare, on the condition that I would pay it him back when I came back. What I didn't know was that he'd been talking to the accounts people at the hospital and had managed to persuade them to give me a loan, so it was them that provided the money.

I bought my ticket to Australia, but while I was waiting to go, I was homeless and had absolutely nothing. I went to the job centre to explain the situation, and they said that I'd have to collect my giro, so I went back at 3pm and waited. At 5pm I was still sitting there, and they were closing up – they told me that they had forgotten to issue me with my money, and I'd have to come back at 9am. I went back the following morning and waited until 3pm, when they issued me with a cheque for £2.30. I cashed it and bought a drink with it. The mentality of bureaucrats is beyond me – that's what it felt like with the authorities, time and again.

I didn't have long before my flight. It was March 1992 and John Major, the prime minister, had just called a general election. I didn't care that I was going to be out of the country for it: I've never felt that politicians or governments have ever done anything to represent me – they've always let me down, and I didn't think voting would make any difference.

The last thing I did before I went was to stay with Margaret and Pete for a week in Harlow, Essex, where they were living. Pete had become a Buddhist, and showed none of his previous inclination towards violence – of course, I was a burly bloke by now, and he seemed small to me. He'd taken on a job as a caretaker for the Quakers in Harlow, and showed me around the town. He still drove me barmy – I couldn't stand the man.

Margaret drove me to Heathrow to catch my flight. I left with not much more than what I was wearing, and arrived in Melbourne at some ungodly hour in the morning. I hadn't told Kevin that I would be coming, so when I turned up he was very surprised. I rang him up at something like 4am.

"Where are you?"

"At the airport!"

"What the hell are you doing here?"

He was stern with me, but turned up with his six-year-old daughter Robin.

"What kind of trouble are you in now?"

"I'm not in trouble – and hello to you, too!"

I sat in the back of the car with Robin as we drove to his house in Gelong, just southwest of Melbourne. His house was quite big – it was a bungalow with a big double garage and a postage-stamp lawn. Inside, there was a long central corridor with lots of rooms coming off it. At the back of the house there was a huge covered barbecue area and an enormous lawn.

I soon worked out that I still had an Australian bank card that I was able to use, so I took out the daily limit of $200. In the past I'd always gone to a bank at a minute before midnight to make a withdrawal, and then made another one just after midnight – in those days, it didn't stop when the card ran out, so I could keep withdrawing money. I got into debt. I ended up overdrawn by $2,000.

A strange thing happened while I was staying at Kevin's house – I received a poll tax bill for £42 from the UK. I'd been homeless, so how I could I end up owing poll tax? But then it clicked – I'd stayed with Margaret in Harlow before I went, so I'd been billed for that week. I don't know how they got my address, but I'd bet anything that it was Pete who told them.

When I arrived, Kevin had assumed that I was in trouble, but that wasn't the case – I'd come back to see him because I missed my little brother and also because I wanted to tie up some loose ends in my life. Kevin's a lovely bloke – although he's also been damaged by the experiences that we went through, he's managed it much better than I have. He had married and started a family, and launched a landscaping and grass cutting business. While I was over there, I did a bit of work for him and he paid me $50 a day. His main contract was with service stations – many of them in Australia have massive lawns and Kevin used to mow them and get $300 cash each time. He could mow six lawns in a day, so he was doing alright for himself. He was a bit cheeky to give me only $50, but then I'd been a bit cheeky to show up without warning and ask him for a job. After I'd bought a loaf of bread and a packet of cigarettes each day I'd be down to $45, but then I did get free board at Kevin's house. He showed me how to use a strimmer and how to remove the guard and make a straight line. I tried it back in England when I came back and took half the lawn up!

While I was there I told Kevin that I wanted to see my ex-wife Helen and son Joshua in Tasmania. We had finalised our divorce while I was in Cornwall, but I wanted to apologise for disappearing, as well as for hitting Joshua and for being a terrible person. I decided to go there by boat – the Abel-Tasman ship across the Bass Strait took more than ten hours and was more expensive than flying, but it was something that I'd always wanted to do and I'd saved a bit of money from my work with Kevin.

As I was going below deck to the bar, I recognised a man coming up the steps – it was Leon Herbig, my probation officer in Tasmania. Of all the people in the world, the first person that I met was him! I went to the bar, ordered a jug of beer and fell asleep in a corner.

I hired a car as soon as I reached Tasmania, but because I'd been away for a while the roads were different from how I remembered them. It took a little while, but eventually I got to Launceston. I went to a pub called The Billabong in the town centre – it had been a long day and I was ready for a few beers. I stayed the night there and drove to where I'd lived with Helen on Bishops Drive the next morning. I took a while to find it, because lots of new estates had sprung up since I'd left. I drove past it a couple of times, and then I sat there for a little while, before I saw movement inside. I knocked on the door.

Helen still lived there, and invited me in. The house was basically the same, but there were a few more kids around. A little dark-haired kid came out.

"Do you remember your dad, Josh?"

He looked at me with a funny expression and said, "Yes," before running off to play.

I spent around an hour there. Helen told me how she was doing, while Joshua stayed in another part of the house – I never got the chance to say anything else to him, and that was the last time I ever saw him. Helen thought it was best not to disturb him – he clearly didn't want to come and talk to me.

Afterwards, I went round to Helen's parents' house at Riverside, where I got an understandably cold reception. I spoke to Helen's brother Ranga about the people we used to know, and then I left. I travelled around the island, going to some places I used to know, before I eventually ended up in Exeter. I went to the garage on the main road near Tresca and met Jason, my old friend from school. He asked what I was doing and I told him that I'd come back to Tasmania to see some old friends. He told me that Noel, my old science teacher, had died, which made me very sad, because he was one of the few people who had been kind to me. I didn't go and find the Richmonds, because I didn't ever want to see them again.

It's clear to me now that I was looking for answers. I hadn't found any in England, but in Tasmania I had seen my ex-wife and child, as well as lots of places I remembered from when I was there before – however, being there didn't solve anything or give me any direction.

A strange thought came to me as I was driving around: maybe I should abandon the car and stay in Tasmania – I could camp out and be a fugitive. I didn't want to go back to England because I felt I belonged in Australia, but time was running out on my visa. Even though I had spent many years in Tasmania, I'd been denied an Australian passport: the stark reality was that I could only stay for three months. I was sad at having to leave, and also that I hadn't yet been able to talk to Kevin honestly about everything that had happened.

Although I didn't know it, Kevin had applied to sponsor me as an employee – if that had been successful, I would have been able to stay in Australia on the condition that he provided me with work. However, the authorities didn't accept the application, and I had to leave Australia. I got the ferry back from Tasmania to the mainland and, after spending another week with Kevin and his family, flew back to England.

15.

STARTING OVER

I came back to England feeling heartbroken and stayed with Margaret in Harlow for a few days. While I was there, I went to see her mum, Ida, who was living in a retirement bungalow – I hadn't realised that she was still alive. I called her Auntie Ida and she told me to call her grandma – but I couldn't do that, because she'd always been Auntie Ida to me and I didn't want her to be anything else. Her husband Alex had passed away in 1986.

I was totally despondent and felt as if I hadn't achieved anything in my life. I headed back down to Cornwall and began drinking heavily straight away. I had no hope for the future and felt that I simply did not belong. My hatred for the authorities got worse and I carried on rebelling, ending up in court several times due to my drink problem. I was seeing a counsellor and they would give me advice on how to cut down, but a voice inside my head would always say to me: "Hang in there, you've just got 15 minutes left and then you can go for a drink." And as soon as the counselling was done I'd leave and go straight to the pub.

This went on for quite a while, up to a point when I became suicidal. I would just go and lie in a road, waiting to be run over. Or I'd climb up a crane, planning to jump off. Looking back on it, some of the things I did seem funny now, but at the time I was feeling really desperate. But no one ever did run me over. And I never jumped.

In despair, I decided to go to the Fairbridge Society, the people responsible for shipping me off to Australia in the first place, and try to get some answers from them. But all they seemed interested in was covering the whole thing up, rather than trying to help me understand what had happened. I was left feeling desperate and despondent. On the way back I talked about my life to a woman on the train and told her what I'd been doing in London. She said something to me about radio – at that point I'd never heard of Radio Cornwall, but I wrote down my address and telephone number for her, and four weeks later I got a call.

This lady had put a message out over the radio saying that I was looking for Bruce, and soon afterwards I got a call from an unknown number telling me to go and meet him at Plymouth Coach Station. It was a horrible day, but I went there and waited under cover. As I was sitting there, a face popped around the corner and looked at me.

"Hello brother."

"Fuck me!" I exclaimed. He'd given me a real fright – he was a smartly dressed man wearing polished brogues, and I was wearing crappy clothes, because that's the way I am.

We shook hands, but it was like meeting a stranger. I suppose that was inevitable after 22 years apart – so much stuff had happened that it was hard to make amends. I didn't want to have to justify our lack of communication or tell him everything that had been done to me.

Bruce looked around edgily. "We'll have to wait here a while – there's something planned."

"Fine," I replied, not having any idea what he was talking about.

We waited, making small talk. Bruce kept looking at his watch, but nothing happened, so we went to a little café and I sat down opposite him. Bruce looked at me and took a deep breath. "Why didn't you reply to any of my letters?" he asked.

I looked at him blankly. "What letters?"

"I sent loads of letters to Tresca, but you never replied."

My jaw fell open. We'd never seen any letters from him – he'd thought we were ignoring him for years, but

Harry and Lily hadn't ever shown them to us. It shows just how determined the Richmonds had been to control us, to deny us any outlet that they could not monitor. Bruce had resented us for not communicating with him – and because he'd been thinking that way for the last 22 years, his resentment had been allowed to fester for far too long.

"We never got them," I said. "Harry and Lily must have hid them from us. We had absolutely no idea where you were."

"I spent years thinking you'd disowned me!"

"You're fucking kidding," I exclaimed.

"I'd appreciate it if you could stop swearing," he said, looking at me.

"Why?"

"I'm deeply religious," he replied.

This wasn't the brother I remembered – I knew him as a mischievous, violent young man, just like me. This man in front of me felt totally unfamiliar, and I couldn't think of how to talk to him without swearing.

He kept on looking at me, and then at his watch, and we stayed for a couple of hours, with nothing at all happening. Eventually, I asked him what we were waiting for. We didn't have mobile phones back then, so we hung around waiting for whatever Bruce had organised, but it never happened. Unknown to me, he'd organised something with Television

South West – he wanted them to film our reunion for the local news – but something had gone wrong and they never showed up. So he went back to where he lived, and I went back to where I was staying. About a week later I still couldn't believe any of this was true. My head just couldn't accept that he was my brother – he was too clean cut and well spoken.

Bruce asked me to go and stay with him at Alphington, just outside Exeter in Devon, and I accepted, because I didn't have anywhere else to go. You have to remember that I had been in all kinds of places, so I was slippery and knew how to evade people – being an alcoholic makes you good at that. He knew that I had a drink problem so he said, "If you drink, you're not staying in this house." I went out that night had a drink and he let me back in. Some rules you've got there, Bruce!

I stayed there for about two weeks, and in that time I helped him dig the foundations for an extension. His house was built on an old truck yard so it was all compacted clinker and we had to dig eight feet down. I'd be outside the back door with my head below ground level, and I wouldn't see him until he got home from work. His wife was very loud, and I always thought of her as being like the fishmonger's wife. She was very strict and insisted that swearing wasn't allowed in the house, but I didn't care and swore like a trooper. I was brought up to swear in Australia – that's the way Aussies are. If you meet someone out in the bush, the first thing that comes out of your mouth is a swear word.

That kind of restraint is not something I like in a domestic setting. Tresca was clinical in the same way, but I like warmth and homeliness and the smells of cooking. Bruce's house felt cold and emotionally sterile – it was scrupulously tidy, his wife went round cleaning the whole time, and we had to say grace before meals, which I hated.

I had to escape from there, and when I did, I really let loose. I got so drunk in Exeter that I smashed a bottle off by the neck and threatened to cut my throat. I was arrested and was taken to hospital where I sobered up. I was only there for a couple of days, during which time I saw a counsellor, but I never told Bruce. I think he was looking for something for me to do – he clearly didn't want me to stay at his house forever – and one day he mentioned that he'd seen a job advertised that he thought I might be interested in. It was in a hotel in Moretonhampstead, in the middle of Dartmoor. The advert simply said, "Hotel staff wanted, Dartmoor." I rang them up and they invited me along for a chat.

Staying with Bruce felt like some sort of regime: I'd get up and dig the bloody trench, then they would make some food, and then we'd sit and pray before going to bed – it was the same routine every day. I had left a country that was free and easy and come back to a place that felt like an institution and reminded me of being at Tresca. However, without Bruce I would probably never have applied for the hotel job – I'm grateful to him in that respect, because the job helped to save my sanity.

I took the bus to Moretonhampstead on a stinking day with the sort of thick, murky drizzle that you only get on the moors. I didn't feel very optimistic about my prospects. I felt out of place – I'd never seen a stately home before. The drive was nearly a mile long, and as I walked up it in my ill-fitting clothes, I thought there was no chance I'd get the job. The only position going was for a kitchen hand – a pot scrubber – but they gave it to me straight away, and suggested that I start the next day. I walked all the way back to Moretonhampstead, got a bus back to Bruce's house, and packed my things. I couldn't wait to leave – I'd had enough of praying at meals, because it's just not my cup of tea – but I did thank god that I had a roof over my head.

The hotel was a massive former manor house with a golf course, and had been owned by WH Smith. When I arrived I was shown to my digs, which were where the drivers used to live back in the old days – little apartments above the garages. My room was comfortable – it had a nice bed and lovely views. It was great, though it did get cold in the winter. There was also a staff bar under the hotel that was run by the head housekeeper. She looked like a dragon and could be hard as nails, but once you got to know her, she was brilliant.

I started working in the kitchen, which was tiring but straightforward, and I got on well with my colleagues. I'd be scrubbing down the far end of the huge kitchen, when I'd hear the chef yelling "Have you done that big pot yet?" and it would still be caked in cooked-on scrambled egg, burnt on the bottom. I'd have to scrub like crazy to wash it and take it to him, and I'd get a real sweat on doing it.

One evening they were short of housekeepers – I leapt at the chance to do something different, and went round changing bedsheets and leaving chocolates on pillows. Soon after that they lost one of their housekeeping staff, so I was asked to help with housekeeping for a week. I had a trolley that I would fill up with sheets and bedding. I didn't realise that upstairs in the hotel the old wooden floors were wonky, and as I trundled over them with my heavy trolley it would make the floorboards rumble and rattle, waking up everybody on the floor below – I quickly learned that you had to move the trolley slowly. It was a quirky place, but the clientele were marvellous, and the tips I received were unbelievable. There was one guest who particularly sticks in my memory. The girls who normally made the beds were busy, so I changed the bedsheets that day. As I left one bedroom, the lady arrived back and gave me ten quid. My eyes lit up – I was really onto a winner here. The guests used to ask me for directions and other local advice, and would give me lots of tips for my trouble. My basic wage was £950 a month, which was around £910 after tax, but my accommodation and meals were provided, and I didn't ever really have to leave the grounds.

The job gave me a real feeling of purpose, which helped me to relax when I wasn't working. In the evenings I would play a few holes of golf on the course or I'd walk around the grounds – all 360 acres of them. Moretonhampstead was just down the road and my brother was miles away, so I didn't have to see him. I felt strange about this, but the truth was that I had difficulties getting on with Bruce and his family because I was so different from them. I was instinctively aggressive towards him, because I felt he'd done the dirty on me by escaping from the Fairbridge people.

I still get angry with Bruce – and I think it's because he was allowed to stay at home and didn't get sent to the other side of the world. I'd like to think that I could have a straightforward conversation with Bruce now, but I can never pin him down. He's evasive, and I think it's because he's afraid of getting hurt – after all, he thought I was ignoring his letters for all those years. And I'm sensitive to the idea of him ignoring me, too. But even though I'm not afraid to tell him what I think of him to his face, we both find it difficult to discuss emotions. If I could have a frank conversation with him I would, but that moment of saying goodbye in 1970 still haunts me.

I absolutely loved working at the hotel, and stayed there for three years. I even won three awards for my work there: two silver medals and a bronze, for excellent service to hotel guests. That may not sound like much, but for almost the first time in my life I was taking real pride in my work and it felt good to be recognised for it. Each year the award-winners were taken to the company's flagship hotel in Manchester, where for three days we would want for nothing. There was a massive ballroom in the basement, with vases on the tables that were about three feet high, with beautiful flowers in them. The cutlery was so well polished that you'd go blind looking at it, and it took me back to when I used to polish the cutlery at Tresca. There was also free food, free booze and fantastic accommodation. All this was our reward for excellence – it was ostentatious, but I also felt that I deserved it.

But one day, rumours started going round that the hotel was being taken over. They turned out to be true, and I was out of a job again. I was sad to leave because I had enjoyed it so much, and I had no idea what would happen next.

I'd spent over a decade writing letters to the Fairbridge Society to ask for more information about my case and about my mother. In 1993 I received a file in the post. It felt like a real breakthrough, but when I opened the file it had black lines throughout the documents, obscuring names, places, and other details. Various letters and statements were plastered with the word "REDACTED".

I discovered very little new information about my mother, but it seemed that dad had been our main carer after leaving our mother in 1960 to live with another woman. After my father died in 1962, we were given back to my mother, but she struggled, possibly with depression, and was unable to cope with looking after three children. Our mum married again in 1962 but she was still unable to look after us, so we were taken into care by Cornwall County Council. We were in a foster home for a few months, until mum made one last effort to try to care for us, under supervision. When that didn't work out we were sent to a children's home in Newquay and then, the following year, we were fostered by Margaret and James Robson. The file also stated that my mother had last been seen in Belgium in 1970, but there was no more detail than that.

I have no memory of either of my parents. When I asked Bruce about those early years, he said he couldn't remember mum or dad either, even though he was eight when dad died. Evidently we'd found different ways to deal with the events of our early lives, and one of them was simply to blank out the bad memories.

The file suggested that we started living with Margaret and James somewhere near London, but I don't think that is likely – how and why would Cornwall County Council have given us to foster parents near London? It's possible that Margaret and James were talking to Cornwall County Council about fostering while they were preparing to move down to Mevagissey from London, but the first time I remember being in foster care was in Rose Cottage, in Heligan Woods, the only place that I've ever really been able to call home. There is nothing in my memory about how I got there, but I remember that for the first year or so we were there, I was living in a kind of paradise.

Heligan Woods are not far from the so-called Lost Gardens of Heligan, which were just overgrown rather than lost when we lived there – but then again, calling them "The Very Overgrown Gardens of Heligan" wouldn't really have had the same ring to it! Those gardens and the woods around them were my playground between the age of five and ten, but today you can rent Rose Cottage for about £1,500 a week. When I lived there it was a humble country cottage, rather than a posh country retreat for people with more money than sense. The man who "found" the Lost

Gardens, Tim Smit, lived in Rose Cottage while he was restoring the gardens; I read his book about Heligan, and the way he describes discovering the gardens brings it all back to me. He describes struggling through a jungle dense with all sorts of exotic ferns, enormous trees and rhododendrons, as though it were Peter Pan's Neverland or the Amazon rainforest, rather than some gardens in southern Cornwall.

Looking back over the Fairbridge file, I found a letter that Harry had written to the director of Fairbridge, Major General Campbell, about my behaviour. It was written in August 1971, 20 months after we had arrived in Tresca.

Re: Rex Wilton

Dear Sir,

I think that you would wish me to write to you and advise you of the activities of Rex Wilton over the past two months. [...]

During a period of three to four weeks, Rex either left home without telling me and was away all night, or did not come home from school but travelled on a school bus for two miles or so and did not come home for the night. There were in all four occasions: twice he failed to return home from school and twice he left home.

On all but the last occasion he was away for just one night and was never more than two miles from home. He slept in a hay barn

*twice and in a garage once. The last occasion was much more serious.
He left home at 8pm, taking a bicycle, and was away for two nights
and almost three days.*

*Rex was eventually traced to Hillwood – a small village on the
east side of the Tamar River, almost opposite Exeter. He had taken
a small rowing boat from the beach and tried to row himself across
the river, almost a mile. He managed to lose an oar and was drifting
when a fishing boat picked him up and took him to Hillwood. He still
had the bicycle with him and he filled his time riding along the roads
and at night slept on the river jetty and in a parked bus, from which he
took a parcel of dry cleaning, a man's suit, and two pairs of slacks,
which he threw into the river. The police picked him up and returned
him home after three days.*

This complaint about my behaviour, with no considera-
tion of its causes, made me think about the Richmonds.
There were only ever five of us children there – I think
Harry and Lily had probably worked out that this was the
optimum number, because it allowed them to operate the
home without additional staff. And I assume that it was
also enough children for them to be paid a handsome
sum in return for housing us – they didn't have other jobs,
so were able to make a living from looking after us. We
were literally their business. I don't know who was paying
them – the home was a Fairbridge home, the Tasmanian

authorities were ultimately responsible for us and the Cornish County Council had sent us over there in the first place, but I don't know which of those bodies contributed.

I have always believed that there must have been a financial reason for us being sent to Tasmania in the first place. I expect that Cornwall County Council or people working there were given some form of backhanders to allow it to happen in the first place. The whole child migration scheme was meant to have ended by 1970, so why did I end up going? I think it was because of corruption – perhaps Harry and Lily needed more kids to keep the home running so they contacted Fairbridge, who gave Cornish County Council some money, and we were sent over. I can't imagine how anyone could play with children's lives like that, as though we were chess pieces to be moved around a board.

16.

CHRISTINE

I suppose I could have used my job at Moretonhampstead as a stepping stone towards something else, towards something better. It was a positive experience that I could have used to gain momentum, but that didn't happen. Instead, I stumbled again and ended up in a mess. Being in a place that was a little like an institution, where I didn't have to think about rent or bills, and where I had easy access to alcohol, might have had something to do with it. When I found myself back in the "real world", it all got a bit too complicated for me. I found myself drinking again, and soon enough I was in trouble once more.

I ended up in a dry house in Exeter, which was halfway between being in a hospital and having full independence. In many ways, I felt that this was the kind of place where I'd been ever since I became an adult – a supervised institution that meant that I wasn't fully independent. Just like St Vincent de Paul, Rashleigh House, and the hostel in St Austell. But the thing that felt slightly different was that I had taken this route myself to try and get better – I had been to the bottom, and was now making a grown-up decision to try and move forwards.

Unlike Bruce's house, the dry house was very strict. It was right in the centre of Exeter on Magdalen Street, an old red-brick terraced building. It was run by a lovely married couple called Paula and David and there were about six of us there. I'd always wanted a room in the attic, and I turned it into my home, with lots of little decorations – because I wasn't drinking and was on benefits, I had money for once, and was able to buy stuff.

Each day I would go out and do voluntary work for the National Trust, and when I came back they'd always ask me if I'd had anything to drink that day. I didn't go out in the evenings – I used to sit and write poetry, or read, or listen to the radio. There was no television in the house, so you had to find something to occupy yourself.

How did the volunteering start? Well, I remember that I would sit in a beautiful cobbled courtyard that had a wonderful oak tree in it. There was a Relate marriage counselling office there, as well as a charity that provided education for travellers. I overheard someone talking about volunteering and when I asked them about it, they told me to go and speak to a dear old lady called Sylvia. At the time I had shaggy hair and filthy clothes, and I stank of alcohol, but they still took me on. The work helped me to feel like I was needed by someone again, and I managed to dry myself out.

When I started volunteering, I met a girl called Wendy. I spoke to her on my first day, and she called me "possum" because of my Australian background. I was always excited to volunteer, because it meant that I could see her. I remember us going to strim the grass at the charity in the summer – we'd take it in turns to work, and when she was working, I'd sit and watch her. I felt pretty lonely at the time, so I kind of attached myself to her. Wendy was interested in my life story, so I gave her the rundown, and then looked at her asked if she would go out with me.

"Sorry Rex, but I'm… er… not particularly inclined towards men," she replied.

I didn't see that coming, but it didn't faze me. We ended up working together for quite a bit, but I didn't tell her that I was an alcoholic and that I was living in a dry house.

I really enjoyed the volunteering, and eventually Wendy and I started meeting in Exeter to go shopping together. Our friendship grew stronger – I knew I couldn't be with her as a lover, but we were still able to have a great relationship. Wendy was a really smart woman and had studied aeronautics. At some point she moved up to Manchester for work and I went to see her. She took me to a basement bar there that was a real eye-opener. I couldn't work it out at first, because it was full of all these gorgeous women and there were almost no blokes. I looked at her, wide-eyed.

"This is a gay bar, Rex," she said.

"I wish I was a lesbian!" I replied.

Soon afterwards, we started seeing a blonde lady coming in and out of the charity offices. I was single, so Wendy asked me, "What about her?"

"I think she's too upmarket for me," I replied.

"What? And I wasn't?" Wendy said.

She went over to ask her out herself, but came back saying, "Her name's Christine, but she's not that way inclined, so why don't you ask her out?"

"I don't bloody know her!" I said. But I gave it a go anyway, and she said yes.

I invited Christine around to my flat. She had German ancestry, but had lived in England for much of her life. I think her background made her more direct than most English people – when she came to the flat and I asked if she wanted a drink, she said, "If I want a drink I'll fucking have one." I made her a coffee and she sat opposite me on the sofa and said, "Well, aren't you going to fucking kiss me?" She was direct to the point of bluntness, and was never scared to say what she wanted. When I first met her, she was running the education bus that I'd seen in the car park – she took it to gypsy camps all over the southwest, where it was used as a mobile classroom. She lived in Broadclyst, near Exeter, rode a red motorbike and had two kids called Harry and Rachel from a previous failed marriage.

We started to get to know each other but it was never a peaceful relationship – there was always tension between us and I suppose I'd describe our relationship as tempestuous, but she was an amazing woman. I went to Germany with her once – we went to Bielefeld near the Black Forest for Christmas and I met her aunt and uncle and the rest of her family. I remember going for a drive with her uncle in his Mercedes. He said that there was a lot of rubbish everywhere in England, but that in Germany the roads and countryside were very clean. Well, as we drove through the Black Forest it was very beautiful, but at one point we came to a clearing that was full of rubbish from a picnic – he was so apologetic and ashamed that I felt sorry for him.

I didn't exactly propose to Christine. I remember her asking me in her usual direct way, "So, when are we getting married?" and I just said "How about next month?" So that's what we did. We got married at a registry office in Exeter in 1997, with just her family and a few friends there. It wasn't a big deal, because we didn't want a fuss. This started a pattern that I would repeat again: I would meet a nice lady with kids from a broken marriage, and would step in. Christine's ex-husband was rude – when he'd turn up to take the kids out, he would stand in the doorway saying, "Why aren't they ready? You should have them ready." However, if I ever told them off she would flare up and shout at me that they weren't my kids. I didn't know what I was supposed to do.

After we got married, Christine discovered a house that had come up for rent in Moretonhampstead – it was one of the old almshouses there. We moved in, and our landlord was the National Trust, who considered the buildings to be of "national importance". They dated back to the late Middle Ages and apparently had been converted into almshouses in the seventeenth century. They were made of solid stone, with a very distinctive porch – or "loggia" as the National Trust called it – that faced onto the road, and a series of beautiful archways. We used to sit in the porch on summer mornings drinking coffee, and on warm evenings we would sit there and share a few beers. Our house had thick walls, lead-lined windows and stone floors. There was an Aga in the kitchen and a back window that looked out on to the garden, a small lounge, three bedrooms upstairs and a bathroom. The building had a thatched roof and it was a wonderful place to live.

While we lived in the almshouse I had a little dog, a King Charles Spaniel called Jacob. I would walk him every day, but things were not all well. I was still being what I would call a "toe-rag" – despite my time in the dry house and the coping mechanisms I had learned to avoid alcohol, I was still drinking too much on a regular basis. One time I got so drunk that I ended up in Wales, without knowing how I got there!

However, my drinking turned out to be the least of our problems. One day, Christine found a lump under her breast, and within weeks had been diagnosed with breast cancer. I supported her through the treatment – we went together to a cancer group, where we met fellow sufferers. When we first went there were seven people in the group, but before long there were only two left. Christine was on Tamoxifen, and had to go in for regular treatment. One day I got home from work to a voicemail message – Christine had collapsed at work and had been taken to the Royal Devon Hospital. I went to see her straight away. She looked terrible, but told me that she was fine – she said she'd been overdoing things at work. And a year or so after the diagnosis, Christine got the all-clear.

At this point, Christine had given up working for the educational charity and had started a job running a chain of charity shops – they were doing really well, and she had been able to keep on working throughout her illness. It felt like she was starting to pick up and have more energy again, but at some point I noticed that there was something different about her – she smelt different, and it worried me. I decided to talk to her about what was going on, and told my boss that I was taking a weekend off. On the Saturday morning, we sat outside the front of the house, having a cup of tea.

"Are you alright?" I asked.

In her usual, blunt manner she simply said, "No, the cancer's back."

"Where?" I asked.

"In my liver."

I hugged her, but it didn't feel right that she hadn't told me, despite knowing about it for weeks. As well as feeling sad and upset, I felt angry and betrayed that she had not confided in me as soon as she had found out.

I tried hard to put all my energies into helping Christine, but I was also working 11 hours every day. She had to go for chemo regularly and I went with her as often as I could. We went to see her consultant and both listened in frustration as he spouted statistics that didn't really mean anything. Afterwards, when Christine had gone to the toilet, I confronted him.

"Treat us like adults and stop talking rubbish. Tell us the truth. How long has she got?"

He looked me in the eye and said, "Three to six months."

My health was going downhill, too – I was suffering under the strain of my home and work life and was still smoking and drinking too much. One day at work in June 2000, while carrying an enormous American fridge up a flight of stairs, I felt a twinge in my back. As the day went on, the pain got worse and when I got back to my digs after the day's work, it still wasn't improving. I eventually rang the hospital and explained the situation, and they said, "If you can get to us, come down." I arrived at the hospital, and they got me a bed and hooked me up to an ECG. I was lying on my back and the pain was so bad that I started to cry. I couldn't see anybody, so I yelled out, "Can someone please help me?"

The next thing I knew I was in the operating theatre having a stent put in – I found out later that one of my arteries had collapsed.

I had a month off work and my boss came to see me every other day. He'd drive 20 miles, bringing me cigarettes and gifts, and told me not to worry about money. A month later, I went back to work.

Five months after that, I was driving my truck from Truro to Exeter when I started to feel hot and sweaty. I knew that something wasn't right.

I was having a heart attack. I pulled in and rang my boss, who said he'd get an ambulance sent out to me. I sat there literally pressing all my muscles together to stop the pain, when an ambulance zoomed past – they'd missed me! My boss rang back.

"Have they arrived yet?"

I told him that it had gone past me, so he made sure they turned around and came back, though they had to carry on for some miles before they were able to. They took me down to Plymouth Hospital and rushed me in and gave me some GTN. Unfortunately, they gave me too high a dose – my head was banging and it felt like it was going to explode.

When I was able to get up, I asked if I could go for a walk. On each level of the hospital in those days was a smoking room! I went there, and it was full of half the cardiac ward. I sat down and had a cigarette and then I went back. And I felt really, really bad. They gave me more medication. Eventually I got out of there, but I was off work for another month.

In the early summer of 2001, Christine began to go downhill rapidly. Her legs were swollen, she was drooling, and she had difficulty speaking. We arranged to have a fortnight's holiday in a caravan, and sent the kids to stay with their dad.

I drove her to the caravan site. I had to pick her up and put her in the bed, because she wasn't able to herself. While we were there, she said to me, "What are you going to do?"

That was the first sentence she'd said in two weeks. And then, on the Saturday, she said, "Can we go home?"

We weren't meant to be going home for another week, but we arrived back at around midday and she sat in her favourite chair in the kitchen. There was an Aga in there and it was nice and cosy, and she liked looking out into the garden.

"Is there anything I can get you?"

She didn't reply.

I went out to cut the grass, but left the door open so I could see her. A little later, at about four o'clock, she hadn't moved, so I took her up to bed and stayed up with her all night. Christine passed away the following morning and despite everything I'd gone through already, it was by far and away the hardest day of my life.

The kids were thirteen and nine at the time and had been staying at their dad's house, because of what was happening to their mum. It was unbearable that cancer was extinguishing the light that had shone so brightly in such a vivacious lady. Their dad had the sad task of telling them what had happened, but I was the one who had to tell Christine's mother.

"What have you done now?" she asked me on answering the phone.

I asked her to come round. It was especially hard to tell her that Christine had died because she had already lost another daughter to suicide.

I rang the doctors to ask what I should do next, and they came round and checked her, and then I rang the funeral parlour. I hadn't realised, but three weeks before Christine had died, a nurse had visited to witness her last will and testament.

I didn't know what to do with myself, so I started cleaning the house. Part of me was thinking that Christine hadn't died and that I had to clean the house so it was tidy when she got home.

"What are you doing?" asked the doctor.

I explained that I was cleaning the house for Christine, and I said, "I've still got the kitchen and the living room to do yet."

"Rex, she's dead."

"No she's not," I said. "She won't be long."

There was a knock at the door – it was a second doctor and the funeral directors.

"What would you like Christine to wear?" they asked.

I had forgotten that she was still wearing her night-clothes. So I got out a long dress – and as I brought it out of the wardrobe, her last will and testament fell out. I didn't know what it was, so I just kicked it back in. They got Christine dressed and took her out.

That was the last time I saw her, and it was horrible.

After they had taken Christine's body away, I closed every curtain in the house and drank myself into oblivion. I just couldn't accept that she'd gone. A couple of days later, I was still lying on the couch, drinking and listening to music, when a local religious couple came round.

"We'd like to say a prayer for you."

"I don't want your prayers. I just want my wife back."

In Christine's last few months we'd been getting into financial difficulties because she wasn't earning, but she had savings that I didn't know about. I hadn't been interested in her money so didn't realise, but Christine's mother became angry with me. She came to the house and said, "Where's Christine's will?"

By that point I'd found it and read it, and she went ballistic at me, because it should have been given to a solicitor without me reading it first. Christine had left specific items to different people, so when I'd sobered up, I packed up the items that people were entitled to. Christine had left me her car, but I gave it away. She had left quite large sums of money for her two children, and I kept out of all of that. Two weeks after Christine's death, there was to be a memorial, and in her will, she had stated that she wanted her ashes to be scattered in a field on the edge of the village. They eventually put a seat there on that same spot, next to the almshouses in Moretonhampstead.

As the executor of the will, I was also responsible for scattering her ashes, and her mother, children, and ex-husband, as well as other friends and family members, came with me. I took the tub from the bag, stepped forward, and sprinkled the ashes into the breeze. The wind caught them and lifted them high into the air.

17.

GROUND ZERO

My first day back at work after Christine's death was 11 September 2001. I'd done an early shift and got home at about two in the afternoon. I turned the television on, and the first thing I saw was two towers. Someone said that a plane had just hit, but it didn't register in my head. Then another voice announced that another plane had hit the other tower. My head still wasn't taking anything in, so I went into the kitchen and made a cup of tea. You know when Orson Welles broadcast *The War of the Worlds* on the radio, and it scared the crap out of a load of Americans who thought it was real? I thought this was like that – just a stunt. But then the news came back on, and it *was* real. The whole world had been rocked by a terror attack.

At that point, I felt like I was approaching my own ground zero – the absolute rock bottom of where I could be as a human being. About a month after Christine had died, I decided that I didn't want to stay on in the almshouse – it was costing me £700 a month in rent, which I couldn't afford with one income, and I didn't need as much space now that the kids were no longer living there. I was on my own again, haunted by memories of Christine and the children.

One Friday I got home and decided to put a notice up outside the house: "House contents for sale." The following day I sold almost everything. Christine's daughter Rachel came round, and I gave her the books that Christine had left for her.

Shortly afterwards, I moved to Cullompton, just up the M5 from Exeter. I had found a tiny one-bedroom flat in a nice little courtyard, and the rent was just £50 a week plus bills.

My boss Dominic was ex-military and would strut around like he was still a sergeant major in the army. He was a good boss, though – strict, but he had a softer side, too. After my move, I wasn't feeling right in the head. I was at work one day, and when Dominic looked in and asked me how I was doing, I said, "I'm just popping out" – and I never went back.

I took myself to the hospital in Exeter and when I explained the situation, they admitted me to the psychiatric unit. I wasn't suicidal, but I'd been sectioned for my own safety. In the centre of the unit there was a courtyard, where there were plants and running water and benches. I lit a cigarette and sat down on a bench to read my book. I was there for hours before I realised that I was cold – I was shivering, and nothing would make it stop. I went inside and made myself a hot drink, tucked myself into bed, and carried on reading. The nurses were very caring and asked how I was.

"I'm okay."

They talked me through the stages of grief and asked me what I was feeling. I said I had been through the anger, but kept on getting stuck on the denial, unable to get beyond it. They were very patient, and kept talking to me about how the stages don't always go in the right order – they could take a long time, but at some point I would move through them all. I couldn't get my head around it, because I didn't want to go through the stages – it felt like a betrayal of Christine to even think about moving on from her death, so when I felt like I was on the verge of moving on, it was almost like I took myself back to square one to avoid betraying her memory.

I was curled up in a chair by the window in a tiny private room, when I looked up and saw a blonde lady opposite me.

"I know you," she said.

Christine was the only blonde lady I'd known in my life, and it was almost like she was sitting there, talking to me. At that stage I was quite ready to believe that it was her.

"We've met before," she said.

"Who are you?" I asked, feeling quite spooked by the whole thing.

"I'm Dominic's wife." Dominic was my boss, so it was still quite weird.

"Are you visiting?"

"No, I'm an inpatient," she replied.

I didn't understand and I couldn't remember meeting her before, but perhaps we had. Her name was Jocelyn and she was a very elegant lady. When I'd left work on that final day, I hadn't told Dominic I was going to the hospital, but Jocelyn let him know I was there. She was there because she'd had trouble with her Prozac medication.

Jocelyn was soon discharged once they'd sorted out her medication, but strangely, she came back to take me out only a week after she'd left. It was a weird experience – I hadn't left the unit for three weeks, because I hadn't been allowed. I hadn't even been able to go home to get a change of clothes, because they were worried that it would tip me over the edge. I wasn't ready to go home yet but I did want to get out of the hospital for an hour, so Jocelyn collected me in her car.

"I just want to go home and get some clothes," I said.

I've never met a tougher woman – she was so strong and kind and helpful. It was only after we had started driving that I realised I wanted her to take me back to the almshouse at Moretonhampstead because in my mind, I was still living there.

It had been a horrible experience, but I was finally able to realise that I lived somewhere else now, and I think that was the beginning of moving forward again. My recovery was a slow process, and it took me at least two years to get better. I was diagnosed with clinical depression and put on medication, and after being discharged as an inpatient I continued to attend as an outpatient.

I didn't have a job, but I did have a bit of money squirrelled away – mainly from the house sale. I worked up the courage to put myself on agency lists as a driver. I got one job doing deliveries, but it didn't go at all well. My first call was to deliver some tractor tyres, which had been packed right in the middle of the truck – this meant that when I got to the delivery address, I had to take everything out and then get the tractor tyres out, before putting everything back in again. It took hours and I only managed three deliveries in the whole day, which was far fewer than I was supposed to do. At the end of the day when I took the van back, the bloke just looked at me and said, "Don't bother to call me again."

After a little while, I moved back to Cornwall. I still had the little car I'd had when I lived with Christine – I travelled around in it and slept in it, too. It wasn't a modern car even then – it was a little red boxy Austin 1100 – but I had nowhere else to go at that point, having run out of options. I lived a nomadic sort of lifestyle for a little bit, just driving around places I knew, trying to get by on what little I had. But I was running out of money and was also feeling very low again. After a little while I ended up at St Lawrence's Hospital in Bodmin where I had been before, but in the secure unit this time. After being treated there for a while, I moved to St Petroc's, a homeless shelter in Bodmin. St Petroc is a very Cornish saint – the story goes that he was the son of a Welsh king who came down to Devon and then Cornwall, and founded two monasteries at Padstow and Bodmin. St Petroc has had a presence in Bodmin ever since then – for over a thousand years – and the St Petroc's Society define their mission as being "to provide accommodation, support, advice, training and resettlement services to single homeless people in Cornwall."

I was still drinking, but not to excess, because one of the things about St Petroc's was that you weren't allowed to be drunk when you were there, and alcohol was completely banned from the shelter, which helped me a great deal. I met some really wonderful characters there and we never had group meetings, which I had always hated elsewhere. We did have chores to do, though – they changed every week, so one week I would have to clean the kitchen, and the next I'd have to clean the lounge. There were never any arguments. I got to know John, the guy who ran the place, really well, and he was a lovely bloke.

I did some good and interesting things at St Petroc's, including landscape gardening. I guess that when you're growing up you don't ever imagine that you'll end up in a homeless shelter – I was in my forties by this point, and what had I done with my life? But I felt less rage against the system by this point – more than anything, I was just a bit sad. I was taking antidepressants, and one day I was walking down the street and I realised that I was fog-brained because of the drugs. I had to go to the doctor's every other day, because they wouldn't give me any more medication than that in one go – as well as the antidepressants, I was also on medication for my heart disease at that time.

"Rex, I thought you'd died!"

It was Benny, who I hadn't seen since before I went to Australia in 1992. He was a mate from years ago and had also fallen on hard times. We had both had our fair share of tragedies – his wife had died of pneumonia at almost the same time that Christine had died. They had two little girls, who are now grown up. I told him what had happened to me and where I was living. Nothing fazes Benny – you could tell him that the moon had fallen out of the sky, and he'd probably just say, "Oh, right". His brother Andrew is really clever and a big cheese at the council. In fact, we used to call him Satellite because he was all over the place – although he was intelligent, he was also very scatty.

I met Benny at a party in the late eighties and got on well with him right away. I used to go drinking with him and knew he was someone I could trust. We were never cruel to each other and he was different from most other people somehow – kinder and gentler and always happy, regardless of what was happening. Anyway, when he introduced me to his girlfriend Jeanny, he just said, "This is my friend Rex", without casting judgement on the fact that I was living in a homeless shelter. I didn't see him again for a while after that – I'm not very good at staying in touch with people and was trying to sort out my problems, without knowing how long that would take.

18.

A Turning Point

I decided that I had to get out of the homeless shelter, but I was struggling with money, which made it difficult to know how to take the next step. I hadn't held down a full-time job for about three years, because I'd been struggling with depression and alcoholism. But while I was living at St Petroc's, I received a letter from the solicitors who were handling the probate for Christine's estate. I opened it up, and there was a cheque for £5,500 – it was basically the remainder of Christine's estate, once everything had been given to her children and other beneficiaries. I didn't want it – after all, what would I do with it? I didn't want to profit from her death, so I just put it in the bank and did nothing with it. Up until that point I had been reckless with money – mainly because of my drink problem – and I didn't trust myself with it now.

I decided to give the money to someone at the shelter who I trusted – a guy called Jeff, who agreed to look after it for me. If I needed anything, I would ask him, and he would give me the money. It worked out fine, for a while. I bought a car – a second-hand white Fiat Panda – so I could get around a bit. Most days, Jeff and I would drive up to places on the coast like Bude or Barnstaple – just to look at the scenery and go for little walks. He was okay, and I got on well with him.

I managed to get a caravan in Bugle, a village in the area nicknamed "the clays" because of all the clay pits, which were mainly disused. It's a funny sort of landscape around there, with massive old pits and huge mountains of old spoil that some people call "the Cornish Alps." In between, there are some lovely bits of countryside – places like Goss Moor, stretches of beautiful oak woods on the way down to the fishing port of Par on the south coast, and lovely rolling hills. Bugle feels a bit like a one-horse town: the railway line runs through it, as well as the main road that connects St Austell to the A30. There are a couple of shops, a pub, a café, and a petrol station, but not much else.

The caravan in Bugle was in a yard that was run by travellers. It only cost me £35 a week. As soon as I saw it, I asked Jeff for the deposit from my money and spent the next three months living there.

Jeff still lived in the home, and he'd come and visit me every now and then because he also had a car by that time. I thought it was a bit strange that he was always broke, and yet he could still afford a car – I began to wonder if he had bought it using my money. Then I arranged for him to live on the same site as me – there were a couple of flats in an old converted toilet block, which were perfectly nice. At some point, I thought about trading my car in and getting another one – or perhaps I just guessed that there was something funny going on. Either way, I went to the bank, and found out that there was no money left in the account – for all this time, he had been siphoning it off and spending it on himself.

The old me would have killed him, but I was mellower now and didn't have it in me to confront him, so I simply decided that I would no longer speak to him. I also felt that there was no practical point in getting violent with him – it would be like trying to get blood of out of a stone, because he wouldn't have any of the money left, and the car wasn't worth anything. I couldn't believe that everything Christine had left to me was gone.

I also had an underlying feeling that what had happened had, to some extent, been my own fault. The money had been left to me and I didn't want it and I told Jeff that – so perhaps I had given him a signal that it was okay for him to have it. Despite all that, I wasn't okay with his stealing from me by any stretch of the imagination. It was Christine's money and I would never be able to forgive him.

So I was plunged back into a financial crisis but it didn't last for long: as all this was happening, I had a visit from a community psychiatric nurse who came to review my depression. She told me that I should be receiving disability benefit, because the depression had made it difficult for me to work. I filled in some forms that she gave me and sent them away – they told me that it could take up to 12 weeks, but that if I was successful then I would also get back pay. It felt like I was finally on the road to getting somewhere.

The psychiatric nurse came to see me quite often, just to check I was okay. She encouraged me to go to counselling, and I started a programme that helped me to open up about my anxiety, my inability to trust people, and my feelings of alienation and worthlessness. As well as clinical depression, I was also diagnosed with post-traumatic stress disorder, which was related to being sent to Tasmania in the first place.

When I wasn't having counselling, I went out most days in my little Fiat Panda. I used to leave the caravan site at about seven o'clock in the morning and come back at six in the evening, having driven for miles – the petrol was cheap, and I didn't have anything else to do. One day I went to the bank and found that there was around £1,200 in the account; I supposed that Jeff must have put some back in. I took a couple of hundred out and bought myself some nice food and also decided to keep some cash handy, just in case.

When I went back to the caravan, there was a letter waiting for me saying that the back pay for my disability benefit had been transferred into my bank account. It also said that I would be receiving £310 each month from then on. This meant that I would no longer have to worry about money, which was a big weight off my mind and allowed me to concentrate on other aspects of my life. For the first time in a long time, I started to become more sociable. There were quite a few other caravans on the site and it was a nice little community.

I also started growing flowers. Believe it or not, I used to drive all the way to a timber yard in Devon to get the wood to make the planters for them. My caravan was close to the drive into the site, so it was quite prominent, and when I started filling the planters up with flowers, people noticed and made nice comments that it cheered the place up and that I had an eye for it – that type of thing. I told them who I was, but I didn't give them my life story. Before I knew it, I was having parties in the caravan. They weren't raucous – I'd buy a slab of beer and people would come round and relax. I carried on learning how to make paper flowers out of crepe paper, which I had been taught to do at St Lawrence's and decided to take up again. I made roses and carnations and soon had a caravan full of homemade flowers. There wasn't a particular reason for making them and I didn't sell them – I just liked having them in the caravan.

My time living in the caravan was an awakening for me and a real turning point in my life. I was financially better off, had a place of my own for the first time in a long time, and was free to come and go without being monitored – I still had the odd beer, but I was in control. I had fun, met some nice people, and started to socialise. I enjoyed feeling part of a small community.

However, it wasn't all fun and games at the site. On one occasion we'd been out for the evening, and when we came back to the site we knocked on the door of an old man who lived three caravans along from me. His car was there, but nobody had seen him for three days, and we'd started to wonder where he was. There was no answer, so we went to the manager, and when he got into the caravan he found the poor bugger dead. He'd been drinking, and when he came back to his caravan he'd fallen, hit his head on the corner of the worktop, and died instantly. Only about a week later, someone else on the site died too – it began to feel like the place was jinxed.

I never told anybody there where I had come from, and as long as I could pay the rent, everything was fine. Some of the other people there were unemployed; some had jobs. About 500 yards down the lane there was a meat factory, where a lot of them worked.

From the caravan site, I used to go on a lot of trips up to Devon – I'd drive around Moretonhampstead and Dartmoor, places I used to go to with Christine. I enjoyed being able to go out, especially since I didn't have worries about whether I could afford to fill the car up or buy a meal. For the first time in years I was actually able to save, and I had something to look forward to each day. I still had problems sleeping in the caravan – I thought about Christine a lot, I thought about how I'd lost contact with so many people in my life, and I thought about what I'd left behind. Christine's death was something that I don't think I ever really came to terms with. Every August since her death, I find myself becoming quieter and less outgoing. I don't intend to do this, but I seem to have an unspoken association between that month and sadness. At the caravan site, when people would ask me if I'd been married, I'd tell them. But then the next day I'd get up, make myself a Thermos of tea and go out for the whole day, because it stopped me having to talk to people about her. It was hard, but talking about her felt too personal for them to understand.

"Why don't you shave your beard off, Rex?"

We joked about it, but the truth was that I couldn't shave my beard off because of the scars that were underneath. Even small reminders of my past made me uneasy, and I preferred to avoid thinking about what I used to do to myself. However, the CPN helped me open up about my experiences, and I even managed to talk to her about the self-harm. I had utterly despised myself when I had done it, and thinking about it now made me feel completely sick.

But the caravan site was really good for me, and I didn't self-harm or drink too much when I was there. I was starting to feel comfortable in my own skin for the first time in many, many years – perhaps even for the first time in my life. At the age of 45, I was beginning to look to the future. I felt that there might still be something to live for – though at this point, I didn't yet know quite what it was.

19.

ANNIE

In 2004 I was still living in the caravan. It had been a good
base for me, but the truth was that I wasn't integrating into
wider society and I only really knew the people at the caravan
site – we'd become a close-knit group. I felt ready to take some
form of step forward and the community psychiatric nurse
mentioned a place called the Armadale House Self-Help
Centre near Wadebridge. It was a drop-in centre for people
with various issues – not just mental health problems, but
all kinds of things. I was still having counselling at the time,
and this was part of me improving my social anxiety. My
community psychiatric nurse rang up and spoke to a lovely
lady called Jane who worked there and got me to go along
– in fact, she sort of bullied me into going, which was great,
because I wouldn't have gone on my own. When I went, I

met Jane in person, and she showed me around the place, including a garden with a greenhouse around the back, which was a little overgrown. On that first day I spent most of my time away from everyone else, because the main room was full of people and I didn't feel comfortable going in there.

My time at Armadale was quiet – at least to start with. I carved wooden mushroom sculptures using a saw and chisels, and spent most of my time working in the garage. I could hear people upstairs, and would go up there to get a coffee or tea every now and then, before going back downstairs and carrying on with my work, or sitting and reading. I didn't feel comfortable integrating with everyone, which is what I was there to do – I've always been shy in front of big groups of people, so walking into that room made me feel really awkward.

I was down in the garage one day, when a woman came down with a cup of tea for me. She had very kind eyes. I thanked her, and watched as she went back upstairs. She had quite a distinctive walk, her shoes sort of clunking as she went, and for some reason that stayed with me. The next day, she did the same thing again. At this point I had a massive beard and long hair and must have looked pretty wild – like some sort of caveman or a Hell's Angel. But Annie told me later that she was able to see through all of that – she says now that all she really saw were my sad eyes.

I think her visits to see me eventually gave me the courage to go and mix with everyone else at the centre. I began to go upstairs, where they would do different types of crafts that people find therapeutic. I started making my paper flowers there, as well as doing other bits and pieces. Annie was always there too, and we got talking a little more. I didn't know any of the details, but knew that she'd come from a horrible mess with her husband. She told me that she'd had a breakdown and was recuperating, and that going to Armadale was a big part of that process. She lived in St Columb, which is on the other side of the A30 from where my caravan was in Bugle. While we were talking, I realised that there was something special about Annie and I started to listen out for the distinctive clunk that her shoes made when she came in and walked across the kitchen floor.

On one particular day, she came down just as I'd got out the lawnmower to cut the grass. I was meeting more and more people at the centre, but I was still spending lots of time on my own, mowing the lawn and carving mushrooms. Annie helped me get the lawnmower out, but as she stood up she whacked her head. I saw tears forming in her eyes and just stood there like a rabbit in the headlights – I had no idea what to do. I didn't even ask if she was alright – I think I just made some inane comment like "You should duck next time." I think most people would have offered some comfort, but I'm clueless about that type of thing, because I was never taught how to react in those situations. So, once I was sure she was okay, I went out to go and mow the grass.

I was soon spending a lot of my time at Armadale. I wasn't there every day, but I did go regularly and was spending more time there than at the caravan park. Annie and I were enjoying each other's company and she introduced me to the joy of smashing glass bottles at the tip, which for her was an enjoyable pastime rather than a boring chore! I think this is where our obsession with going to rubbish tips together started. I loaded up the car.

"Where are we going?" she asked.

"To the tip."

"Oh, you know how to please a girl, don't you?"

But it really did please her. Part of the reason for this was that, in those days, they used to sell things that people had dropped off – for instance, you could buy a chest of drawers for a pound, or a mirror or a shovel for 50p. I absolutely loved this – and was able to kit myself out with a complete set of garden tools for just a few quid.

At around the same time, a woman called Alison arrived at Armadale. We all thought that she was a new member of staff, but she was actually a volunteer "befriender", who was there just to talk to us. It was amazing – she was a very caring woman and helped me to understand a lot about my situation. In some ways she reminded me a bit of Margaret. Talking to her about my life felt like the start of my new beginning.

One day, after talking to Alison about my situation, I found myself in tears. I was still so confused about where my life was heading and felt shaky and uncertain, despite the better direction that my life seemed to be going in. However, there was then a staff shake-up at the centre and it was taken over by a larger organisation, which meant that it would no longer be a drop-in centre. I was sad about this, because I had got so used to going there – and I was worried that if I just went back to the caravan at Bugle it would feel like a step in the wrong direction. I think Alison sensed this, because she mentioned to me that she had a place on her land that I could rent – it was £40 a week, with water from a borehole. Electricity was the only extra cost.

I went round to look at the place, a one-bedroom flat in a nice little converted barn in the grounds of a mill called Old Zanzig, halfway between Wadebridge and St Columb. I decided right then and there that I would take it, so when I got back to Bugle, I told the people from the caravan site that I was leaving.

Old Zanzig was very different from the caravan site
– it was a very peaceful, secluded, and beautiful spot
that was hidden from the main road, with coppiced
woods and a pond. Being there gave me a lovely feeling
that you only get in certain places – a good, settled
feeling. The most noticeable noise there was birdsong.
Alison was married with two teenage kids, and they all
lived in the big house. She took me under her wing and
was a lovely, pleasant lady. She'd get angry about things
sometimes, but never with me.

I was spending lots of time with Annie by this point.
We used to go for walks all over the place together, whatever the weather – there was even something nice about
going out for walks in the pouring rain with her. She had
a wonderfully dry sense of humour and our friendship
blossomed in the outdoors. We had picnics down country
lanes, sitting next to muck spreaders and drinking cups of
tea from a thermos flask. We had both come from such
misery, and yet we found happiness with each other.

I talked to her about Christine. I talked to her about
my life in Australia. And eventually, I asked her out on a
date. Even though we'd known each other for quite a while
at this point, I was still nervous – it felt like a big step to ask
Annie out officially. I asked her son Ian, who's known as
Eebie, if he minded me taking his mother out.

"As long as you don't hurt her," he said, with sadness in his voice.

I still didn't really know the history of what had happened to her at this point – I thought it best not to ask quite yet.

I got dressed up in a brand new white shirt that I had bought specially for the occasion. Eebie took our photo in the archway outside Annie's house in St Columb, and we set off for Trebarwith Strand, a beach that's just over two miles away from Tintagel, on the north Cornwall coast. It's a lovely spot, with sands that are covered at high tide and beautiful rocks and cliffs that you can look down on. The plan was to go to the Port William Hotel that overlooks the beach, but I had some difficulty finding it – probably because I was feeling a bit nervous about the whole thing.

We set off, heading towards Camelford. I'd been there once before and could remember the road in my head, but Annie had never been that way. I just kept driving and driving, until eventually I realised that we was lost. When we finally came to exactly the same place we had started, I felt stupid and angry with myself. So Annie, in her usual, calming way, said, "Let's have a cup of tea," and got her Thermos out. I was still a little upset with myself because I'd meant to be taking this woman out on a date and all I'd done was go round in a complete bloody circle.

But we got there eventually, and had a lovely meal of fish and chips overlooking the ocean, in a restaurant that had a parrot and a fish tank. I could hear the sea and the wind, but most of all I could hear Annie, a lovely lady with a kind ear who was a good listener.

Annie never once criticised me – or anybody else, for that matter. She hasn't got a mean bone in her body; I so admire her for all she's been through, and for the time she still has for others, despite this. She saw me and extended her compassion to me, and it takes a very special person to be able to do that. Our first date was a beautiful evening that I will remember forever – it was romantic and special and it both cemented our relationship and transformed it into something new and wonderful.

I got a new job while I was living in the house in the woods at Old Zanzig, which was where I met the guy they call "Dishy Dave", who's still a friend of mine today. I had decided that I wanted to do some work – I wanted more purpose in my life and felt confident that I was mentally able to manage it. I went to the job centre and asked if I could work and keep my benefits, and was told that I could earn £120 per week while retaining them. I saw a job advertised for a gardener at an exclusive hotel and spa just outside of Wadebridge called Hustyns and decided to go for it.

I told Annie that I had applied for the job and went to have an interview with the head gardener, Bruce Julian. Hustyns is set in 360 acres of beautiful grounds, so Jules and I got in a golf buggy and drove round them, as he explained this and that, then took me back to meet some of the other lads who worked there. He showed me the greenhouse, where he said I would start work, and introduced me to the gardener.

I began a week later. I did three days a week, in no set order or arrangement. I had osteoarthritis by this point, and it was affecting my knee badly. So for the first three days I sat on my backside, tending to seedlings in the greenhouse. I was still a smoker at that point, and every five minutes I left the greenhouse to have a cigarette and cool down, before going back in to start again. Then I realised that there was no need to sit in the greenhouse, and so I started doing the seedlings outside. I got to know Phil, the greenhouse gardener, and we enjoyed working together, sharing a lot of jokes.

It was such an enjoyable job that I genuinely couldn't wait to go to work each day. When I learned that I could use the golf buggy to get around, I was in it every day, shooting round the estate and collecting rubbish in the back. I would stop and talk to guests whenever I could and just enjoyed being happy and sociable. All this time

I had been dating Annie – I would talk to her about my job and she would tell me about what had happened at her work that day.

Hustyns had a pond with a musk duck that we all called Hissing Sid – if you went close to him he would hiss at you, even if you were just trying to give him food. There were also lots of deer on the estate, as well as 50 or so lodges – brick-built, luxurious places that were worth up to half a million pounds each. For the first time in my life in that job, I was communicating with the public. The guests would ask me about the flowers or for directions, and I learned how to get along with people and be part of a group. I did sometimes get told off, but it didn't matter as much to me anymore. I established a pretty regular routine whereby before I started the work I'd actually been assigned for the day, I would make a cup of tea and then get a broom and tidy up the beds, where blackbirds had sprayed wood chippings all over the place. I did many other jobs too, including cleaning the decking with a power washer, maintaining fences, and cutting hedges, but it was all a complete pleasure and I felt like I was in my element. The estate was a little village in its own right, so we never felt isolated and I mixed with all sorts of people from all echelons of society. The job helped me learn not to think about other people as higher or more powerful than me:

instead, I began to think of other people simply as human beings with feelings.

Things had settled down nicely for me. I had never forgotten what had happened to me earlier in my life, but it felt like it had faded into the background slightly. However, it was at this point, in 2005, that something happened to remind me about it in much more detail.

I had written a letter to the Tasmanian authorities through the Child Migrants Trust, and in 2005 a man rang me from the trust and said that he'd like to interview me to learn more about my story. We met for a coffee in Plymouth, and shortly after that, I got a call from somebody called Ian. I sat in the car park at Tesco's talking to him on the phone – and we talked a bit about my history. He told me that the Tasmanian government were paying up to $60,000 in *ex gratia* payments – a term that literally means "out of goodwill" and refers to money paid when there is no legal obligation – to child migrants who had been in care in Tasmania, as redress for childhood abuse. After these initial assessments, I received a letter from the Tasmanian authorities asking for more information – they said that either they could do a telephone interview, I could write a letter, or I could record my story. In the end they sent me three cassette tapes, and I got hold of a tape recorder and told my story.

20.

THE TASMANIA FILE

So I've told my story before – I spoke it into a machine that recorded my words, before sending it to the other side of the world on the exact same journey I made at the age of ten. And then over in Tasmania, those words were listened to by the people who were assessing my claim. It felt strange that I would not speak to them directly – there was no back-and-forth and no face-to-face contact. It was just me talking on tape, with no right of reply. The idea was that they would assess my story and give me an amount of money based on how badly they felt I had been treated. The compensation was "up to $60,000", but I thought it was offensive and should have been $60,000 or nothing for everyone – I mean, how can you put a price on suffering?

In 2006, I was awarded \$47,250, which equated to just over £18,000. I went into the bank in Bodmin one day and got a bank statement from a cash machine, but didn't have my glasses with me. I thought the balance was £190 at first, and it was only later that I realised I had £19,000 in there.

It may sound like a lot of money in some ways, but in other ways it was a drop in the ocean. It was more money than I'd ever been paid in my life, but I still think that given what happened and how it affected my life, it is essentially meaningless. I'm not a greedy person – whenever I've had money, I haven't known what to do with it.

But this money came at a good time for me. I was able to get a new car. I was on benefits at the time, so I declared it – I went to social security and told them, and I told the DVLA. They both said that it wouldn't have any impact on my status, because it related to something that had happened when I was a child and so I couldn't be sanctioned for it. That would also be the case if I got further compensation from the British government.

The money is not the point – the point is that I felt like I deserved the recognition that bad things were done to me. I'd just like people to concede that, take responsibility, and apologise for it. Even starting the process was traumatic for me, and brought all kinds of memories that I hadn't thought about for a long time flooding to the surface, but I felt that I really didn't deserve to be treated like I was sniffing around for money. The Tasmanian authorities did not show any actual remorse for what happened – they just awarded me a sum of money. And the money was treated with suspicion by the authorities in England, who soon used it to challenge my benefits, despite what they had said initially.

When I told the council that I'd been awarded compensation by the Tasmanian authorities, a lady came to visit me. I had spent £1,200 of the money on a second-hand car. It wasn't a good car – second gear wasn't working, so I had to buy a new gearbox for the bloody thing, which ended up costing another £700. Then I bought a music player that cost £199, and that was about it. I was hardly living in luxury; in fact, a lot of the furniture I had at home was stuff I had made out of cardboard.

I gave the lady a cup of tea, and she sipped at it.

"I see you've blown all the money already on that new car," she sniffed. "What else have you spent it on?"

I told her how much the music player and car had cost, and showed her my bank statement to prove it.

"Based on the sum that was paid out to you by the authorities, we're no longer in a position to cover your council tax."

"But I've already spent the money!"

"What you do with your money isn't our responsibility," she replied coldly.

They did stop paying my council tax but I put in an appeal, explaining everything that had happened and producing receipts, bank statements and whatever other paperwork they might need. It took 12 weeks, but I eventually got the money for backdated council tax, and the woman was sacked from her job.

I asked the Tasmanian authorities to send me the full file with all the information that they had processed about me, including their assessment. They sent it over to me, and when I read it, what they had written made me so angry. It was riddled with inaccuracies and untruths and I couldn't believe my eyes. It painted my complaints as trivial – "He did not like the clothes he was given at Tresca" – ignoring the fact that my belongings had been taken away from me when I arrived. It also tried to undermine my allegations of violence, claiming that I had "probably stolen" from the Richmonds. It favoured Harry's accounts of life at Tresca over mine, mentioning my "emotional deprivation", but only as an afterthought. They focused largely on my misbehaviour, rather than the reasons for it.

The whole thing concluded with a recommendation, which stated:

I recommend that this claim proceed. However I have concerns regarding exaggeration by the Claimant and I am aware that there have been varying reports on the Richmonds. The impression from the welfare file is that they were fond of the Claimant and that he ran hot and cold in his attitude to them. In interview with another Claimant [redacted] who was also at Tresca, an unsolicited comment was made that Rex Wade was the Richmonds' favourite. There is also reference on the file to the Claimant's brother Kevin speaking to the Claimant about his rudeness to the Richmonds.

The result of it all was that they were prepared to give me some compensation; they wrote separately that "the State is satisfied that material aspects of the Claimant's allegations have been *prima facie* substantiated as true".

In other words, they had determined that I was telling the truth, despite the insinuations that I was exaggerating and had been a nasty piece of work from start to finish.

Then I received a letter from the premier of Tasmania Paul Lennon. He wrote:

On behalf of the Government and the people of Tasmania, I want to express my deepest regret that this abuse occurred to you while you were in the care of the State. It should not have happened. Nothing you did caused what happened to you and I can only say that I am sincerely sorry. The government recognises the distress, alienation and hurt that you have suffered as a result of this abuse. While the Government is not legally obliged to do so, I believe we have a moral obligation to acknowledge what happened to you and admit that it did occur.

In some ways this meant a lot. There may have been a strong undercurrent of distrust in the assessment, but I was pleased to receive an admission that bad things had been done to me, which until that point no one had ever admitted.

I wrote a letter of thanks to the administrator who had gathered everything together for my claim, and told her about my experience. Bearing in mind that I wrote this letter before I had seen my file, and had yet to discover the way in which the process had been handled, I think it shows how I was feeling at the time:

Firstly, can I thank you for all the work you have done on my case. It has been a long time to get to this stage and I wait anxiously to receive my file.

When I do receive it, I hope to fill in the gaps of my life, to discover some truths, and most importantly some semblance of order.

I cannot express how stressful this has all been over the months to me. I've so much wanted to finalise everything, and now thanks to you, the ombudsman and your department, it can be.

Even after all these years living in England I still remember my life in Tasmania, the wonderful memories and the sad. It always comes down to the question, why?

That fades particularly slowly and I still suffer nightmares about Tresca, but I have learned to live with it.

I am now 47 and suffer from heart disease, depression and anxiety. I see a counsellor for regular two-weekly sessions. It all helps me to come to terms with my former life.

Sorry I have rambled on. I sometimes cannot believe that a government such as yours has recognised now what really went on, and to them I am also grateful.

I wish I could be in Tasmania, so I could thank you all personally, and shake your hands. My deepest respects to you.

Once again, thank you for all you have done to date.

Kind regards,
Rex Wade

21.

SETTLING DOWN

It felt like a big thing to have received the decision and the compensation from Tasmania, partly because it gave me more independence. It meant that I didn't have to worry about whether I would be able to afford to pay my rent, which was £40 a week, or to buy any essentials. And that gave me the opportunity to think more meaningfully about the future. There was one obvious question to answer, but it was going to require a lot of thought.

I had been getting on well with Annie's kids. The stress of the Tasmanian claim had put me under a lot of pressure, and getting it out of the way was a huge weight off my shoulders. I kept on living in my own place, but I began to spend more and more time at Annie's house in St Columb. I loved her, but I was fearful about the size of the responsibility I was taking on – a new partner, with three teenage kids. It felt like a real challenge, and I think I had a bit of a crisis when I was coming to terms with the idea. After living on my own for quite a long time, I suddenly had to face up to the idea of life with three kids. I'd previously been in a relationship where there had been two kids, but these were older – at college or finishing school.

There was also the background of what had happened with Christine. It had taken me years to get over, and I think I had a deep-seated fear about what would happen to me if I took this leap and Annie died as well. I had been forced to think back over my whole life while I was going through the Tasmania case and I wondered how different my life would have been if I'd been brought up differently. But because of the way I had been brought up, and the things I'd done and seen, I had not had a happy life. Looking back on my life, I realised that I was lucky to have made it that far – between the ages of 26 and 30, when I'd first came back from Australia, I had really struggled.

While I was having an argument with myself about whether or not to ask Annie to marry me, she was still on some pretty strong medication that would knock her out for quite a long time whenever she took it. I would take her out somewhere, and the next day when I went round she'd have no recollection of where we'd been.

"What did you do yesterday?" I'd ask her.

"I didn't go anywhere."

"Yes you did. We went to Barnstaple."

I struggled with that side of it, but I kept my patience and watched as she got better and came to terms with her own issues.

But getting married – could I really cope with committing myself like that for a third time? I had to think about it long and hard, but when I did, I knew that I had found a unique person in Annie, and that we had developed a precious bond. I understood then that there was only one thing to do, and I did it a rather strange way. I couldn't kneel because of my bad knees, so over the breakfast bar at Annie's house I took out a silver bracelet instead of a ring, before at the last minute I realised I had forgotten something. So just as I was about to pop the question, I muttered "bugger" under my breath and told Annie that I had to make a quick call.

I walked out of the room and rang Annie's dad. I had already told him that I'd been married before, but he is quite blunt and I was a bit nervous about talking to him, so I just said, straight up, "I'm ringing to see if I can have your daughter's hand in marriage."

He jokingly replied, "She's your problem now!"

I felt a surge of joy and relief as we laughed.

I went back in and Cathy, one of Annie's two daughters, had come into the room, but I couldn't put it off any longer. I sat Annie down and got the bracelet from my pocket.

"Will you marry me?"

Cathy screamed and cried and Annie went a bit strange for a moment, but then she smiled and said yes.

I decided we should do something different with some of the money from Tasmania. I booked tickets for a ferry to Ireland and Annie booked us a cottage. This was a sort of honeymoon, which we had decided to have before we got married. We took the ferry from Pembroke in Wales to Rosslare, and then drove for a couple of hours to a small place near Clonmel. When we eventually found the cottage, we were shown round by a man who talked to us like we didn't speak English, enunciating all his words very carefully. It was bizarre. The night when we got there it was dark, but when we woke the next morning, the light was streaming into the cottage and it was beautiful.

We actually had two honeymoons, but this was one was really special, because it was the first time we had been away together on our own. We went out every day, and I wore shorts, t-shirts and flip-flops, while everyone else was all wrapped up in coats.

We did a lot of travelling over there. Annie had friends called Mick and Sandra who lived near Clonmel, so we spent a lovely week at their place. We went down to the coast one day and it was so cold that there was snow on the hills. I remember seeing a drunk postman delivering the post and swearing at everyone as he veered across the street on his pushbike. One day we went into a café where the radio was on, and the presenter couldn't stop saying "feck this" and "feck that" – it made me think that I might get on alright in Ireland, given how much everyone there seemed to swear!

One day we went to Waterford and visited the crystal factory, famous for making glasses. The scenery around there was beautiful, and as we drove around the countryside, we saw all sorts of ornate gates and long drives leading to big properties in the distance. We also passed disused service stations where they'd kept the petrol pumps and turned them into flower gardens – it was like something out of a weird dream, but we enjoyed ourselves so much.

On the ferry back home, I decided to get rid of my remaining euros on the slot machines while Annie slept, but I kept winning more than I was spending. I wasn't proud of myself and realised that I should have been with Annie on the boat rather than gambling money on those stupid machines. I don't know what it was, but for some reason I was concerned. Perhaps it was the idea of commitment that was now looming over me. The sea was rough that day and I felt that we should have waited and travelled the next day when it was calmer. But we got back to Wales without any problems, and Annie drove us back.

After the Severn crossing, the road divided, and Annie had a forgetful moment and drove the wrong way, towards Bristol. For some reason, that threw me and I panicked and shouted at her as we missed the turning. It was so stupid of me. We'd had a beautiful week and I was worried that I'd spoiled it.

We arrived home in the small hours of the morning. I was still terrified that I'd ruined everything with Annie, and realised how horrible I had been to her. I didn't ever want to do that again and I was worried that she would have been better off without me.

"I saw right through it, didn't I?" Annie says to me now. We met up a couple of days after we got back from Ireland. I apologised for my meltdown and we forgot about it, and got ready for the wedding.

"Oh, Rex, you were hard work in those days," she tells me. "You're much more easygoing now compared with what you were like then. You were like a blooming volcano – you would just explode and I never knew what had happened. You hated yourself when you couldn't control your temper. But then, over time, you changed."

I'd given notice at Alison's house and had started packing up. In the meantime, I had been commissioned to make paper flowers for a wedding in London for a friend of Alison's daughter.

I also made paper flowers for our own wedding. We tied the knot on 3 July 2007 at Bodmin Registry Office, and it was absolutely wonderful. The place was beautifully arranged, with a little garden at the back. Annie's sister came along to be my "best man" and Bruce was there too, though sadly Kevin couldn't make it. Our wedding song as we left the office was "Congratulations", and I remember looking at Annie and thinking how adorable she was. I was smitten, but I was nervous, too.

After the ceremony we drove to Mellingey Mill, a working water mill in the middle of nowhere, for our reception. We had about 30 people there – we didn't want anything that was over the top. The lady who owned the mill supplied the wine, a buffet and tea and coffee. We had a beautiful meal, and the atmosphere was wonderful. The room was decorated with my paper flowers, which had taken me a week to make. Upstairs there was a bar and a lounge, where we cut the cake and made the speeches. What I didn't realise was that the kids had taken bets on how long it would take me to start crying – and when I started to give my speech I could only get as far as thanking everyone for coming before I cracked up and couldn't carry on!

After the reception I went to my old flat, packed up my carful of belongings, and drove to Annie's house at St Columb. I parked in the driveway and didn't unpack it – we only had time for a cup of tea before setting off on our second honeymoon.

We had rented a bungalow in Penzance, and on a good day you could see all the way to the Isles of Scilly. Sadly, we didn't have a single day of good weather while we were there – it was foggy the whole time, so we pottered around but didn't go very far. We looked in the windows of estate agents and thought half-seriously about moving to Penzance. It was a wonderful three days. Our car had been covered with "Just Married" stickers and balloons, which meant that we got tooted at everywhere we went. We drove around the area a little bit, but the weather was against us. We tried to go to Scilly for the day, but even though we couldn't – the fog was too thick for the boat to sail – the bungalow was so comfortable that we didn't really mind. After three days our honeymoon was over, and it was time to head back to St Columb and make a home together.

As we wended our way down country lanes, I had a slight feeling of anxiety about settling into a strange house that I'd never slept in before. My car was parked outside, and was packed with everything I owned in the world, and I had the sudden realisation that I would not be able to do the things I used to do – like get up in the morning and make flowers at my desk or listen to music whenever I wanted. It felt funny at first, because I was used to being out in the sticks, and here I was in a small town, feeling hemmed in. When I first moved in, life was not a complete bed of roses from day one – the biggest problem was that I was grumpy. In the house I'd get cross about little things like people leaving cups in the sink without washing them up. There was no reason for me to react like that, but I felt that it was because of Tresca – where absolutely nothing was allowed to be out of place. I had an innate fear of disorder, because of my fear of what Harry and Lily had done to us when we didn't keep everything clean. I had not lived in a big house since I'd been at Tresca. I got angry and shouted at Annie sometimes, and then regretted it enormously afterwards and apologised.

I think another reason for my grumpiness was the fact that I'd completely given up alcohol. I'd started to drink less in 2000 but still occasionally had a few beers, and every now and again I would get properly drunk. Then something happened that made me stop for good. When I was living at Old Zanzig, I had been out to the pub for a couple of drinks one night and I thought I'd drive home. I came round the corner but misjudged it, came off the road and hit a tree. If I hadn't hit the tree, I'd have carried on down the hill, but because I did I was thrown forwards into the steering wheel. The police came and didn't breathalyse me until I got to the hospital, at which point I was under the legal limit. On my way back to Zanzig, a car pulled up beside me, and it was Annie, with her sister and her sister's son in the car. Her sister, who had never met me, said, "Why are you picking up a tramp?" And that was the last time I ever got drunk.

Drinking had been my crutch – I drank because I wanted to be on my own in my own world, and not in anybody else's. By the time we got married, that had all changed, so I decided to go cold turkey. Stopping drinking was the biggest eye-opener I'd ever had, because I was suddenly able to see the world through clear eyes. There were difficult realities to face up to, but it was also revealing in good ways, because it helped me to see that there isn't always pain, that there isn't always anger, and that there isn't always hatred. It took me a while to clean myself up completely – I started to cut my hair and shave my beard regularly. I liked living somewhere warm, with a doorbell that worked. And we had a dog called Bobby that I would take out for walks.

Now, I only have a beer about twice a year, when we have a barbecue – I didn't even drink at our wedding. Since giving it up, the most I've had in one go was three pints with the people from Hustyns. Annie and Eebie waited up to see me when I got back. They were curious to see me when I was drunk, but I disappointed them – I just said something like, "I had a lovely evening and now I'm going to bed."

It's all about moderation for me now, because I've got more important things going on in my life. I've got a lovely family – that's the most important thing to me, and I don't want to make a mess of it. Besides, I take various types of medication and lots of them don't react well with alcohol, so it's easier for me just to skip it. There's also the fact that having been an alcoholic for 30 years, I've lost around 75 per cent of my liver through disease.

Life hasn't suddenly become simple for me: I still wrestle with my demons on a daily basis, and soon after I moved into the house at St Columb with Annie and her family, it occurred to me that part of my problem was not ever knowing whether I'd done the right thing in life – I'd grown up being told what to do and without the freedom to make my own decisions. Was it right for me to be helping out with three teenagers when I had so little idea of how to bring up children? They always gave me a lot of respect, but I always felt tense, and if someone said the wrong word, I'd fly off the handle. I hated myself for it and was always so sorry afterwards. My anger issues were difficult to get past – I would shout, slam the door, or leave the house and drive off somewhere. It would slowly build up over time and then I would erupt, just like that. I hate myself when I'm like that, because it takes me back to when I would flare up and just hit somebody. I am never violent now, but I still knew that everybody found my anger upsetting. However, I stuck at it, and began to make progress with the whole family. Slowly, I began to feel that I was integrating.

I retired from the hotel at Hustyns soon afterwards, but after three months I went back to work there because I liked the sense of purpose that the job gave me and enjoyed the companionship. Then after another six months, on the advice of my orthopaedic surgeon, I retired again. Then I had my new knee fitted and went through a long period of not being able to do anything. But once I'd recovered, I couldn't stay still, so I went back yet again.

To top it all off, because I was on benefits but was allowed to earn £120 per week, I went to apply for mortgage and council tax relief, before getting a letter to say that they wouldn't give me council tax relief because I was earning a penny over the threshold. It felt like such a jobsworth thing to do, so I rang them up to ask what was going on. That was basically the last straw for me – I decided that it would just be more sensible to give up the job altogether. I managed to get my Disability Living Allowance and I was on income support.

Annie was diagnosed with ME, so I helped her with that and went to classes with her. Some days her energy levels would be fine and she'd work away in the garden, and when I'd bellow "You'll get tired!" out the window she'd tell me she was fine, but then she'd sleep through the whole of the next day. I wanted the best for her, but it took several years for me to learn how to express that.

After I gave up the job at Hustyns I felt like I ought to do something else to give me purpose, so I started to spend my days cleaning and cutting the grass verges in St Columb. I bought myself a petrol strimmer and a lawnmower and got to work. I wore a helmet and a high-visibility jacket. One day, the lady from two doors away walked past.

"Hello Shirley!"

"Oh, Rex, it's you! I thought you were the council!"

I explained to her that I was just doing my bit to make the place look nice. For eight years I did the cutting, I picked up litter, and I planted daffodil bulbs. A nice surprise was that local people raised money – about £430 – to pay me for what I had been doing. The council also chipped in to pay for the daffodil bulbs, but of course, they didn't give me cash: I had to ring up a councillor, who'd take me to a nursery and buy the plants with me.

If I do something publicly, it's because I'm trying to make a difference. Annie sometimes says to me that I should stop, because people will spoil it, but I get a lot of satisfaction out of being able to hold my head up and say, "I did that". Sadly, vandalism became a problem in St Columb: people started pulling plants out and sticking them on top of cars, putting planters in the ditch, and smashing signs that I'd made. After two years of this, I got really cross. When the area had been neglected, nobody had batted an eyelid, but as soon as I'd tried to make a difference someone wanted to mess it up and take it back to how it was.

Once the vandalism started, I felt like I was just wasting my time. It felt like the story of my life – whenever you try to do something good, someone shits on you. I got angry and frustrated, but then I'd go home, get the mower or the strimmer out, and sort things out in the garden.

In 2013 I received the Citizen of the Year award in St Columb, which felt like a real recognition of my hard work. It was the first time they had given the award, and they told me that they planned to award it every year from then on. I got a letter asking if I would attend the council offices. I knew the reason, so I told a few friends, who all agreed to come along. We arrived to find that there was a council meeting taking place, and my award was the first thing on the agenda. I got a few cheers, but before I knew it, they'd moved on to discuss the roadworks on the high street! That was it. I had to go back to the council offices for a photoshoot for the award the following week. I mean, arse about tit. I gave up on the council entirely after that.

I don't trust the authorities, I don't trust local councils and I don't trust the government, because they make all these stupid promises and where has it got us? Nowhere. To the council, I'm like the shit on the bottom of their shoe and it makes me so angry – Annie tells me to lay off them, but I'm fed up with it. Do they want my blood? I'm sorry that as a result of my experiences with social welfare as a child, I began to detest all kinds of authority, and I've never recovered. But I can't believe what I hear sometimes. Don't make promises to me if you can't keep them.

At St Columb, I did the work on the street, looked after the house, and helped Annie get through college and university. She had decided to do an arts degree, starting with a foundation course followed by a BA at

Cornwall College Camborne. She put in a huge amount of effort and overcame all her problems – and I backed her every step of the way. I am so proud of her – she did so much in those seven years or so, and when she got her BA it was the icing on the cake. The graduation ceremony was in Truro and I was delighted for her. She was working so hard that I needed to find something to do as well, so I started to do NVQs in computers, maths and English – and I enjoyed every minute of it.

I don't have many regrets about these years, but I do often think about how many lovely people I've met in my life and not gone back to. Because I've spent a lot of time in Cornwall, I sometimes bump into people who I know and feel guilty that I haven't done more to keep in touch with them. I think it's partly because I spend so much time battling my own demons and have very little time left to think about other people. I recently bumped into the cook from Rashleigh House, who I'd known when I was there during my first time back from Australia. I saw her at the checkout at the supermarket in Bodmin. She remembered me, and seemed really chuffed to see me – she hadn't changed at all, and we stood and chatted for ages.

For the 11 years between 2007, when we got married, and 2018, when we moved, I had what you might call a pretty idyllic life in St Columb, with the children, the pets, and the house. I enjoyed my life there, but it wasn't my home – it was Annie's, so when her two daughters left home, we decided to move away and find our own place where we could spend our life together.

We found a nice little bungalow in Gothers, a little village at the top of the clays area, and moved there in July 2018. It's not far away from St Columb and Bugle, where I lived in the caravan, is just a few miles to the east. There are some remnants of the old clay industry around there, but it's mainly just fields and moorland and woods. It's mainly very peaceful, though we are on the flight path for Newquay Airport so quite a few planes fly overhead. We're pretty much right in the centre of Cornwall, halfway between St Austell and Newquay. It can be quite moody up here – some days the mist settles in and doesn't shift all day.

I haven't been idle here – we've spent a lot of time sorting out the garden together, which is massive. It had been well looked after by the people who were here before us, but we wanted to do something a little different with it – to turn it into an enchanted, unique place that was just for us. Annie has an incredible collection of gnomes – there are about 400 of them, in all – so we set about making space for them, while respecting all the brilliant and unusual plants that were already growing there.

Cynthia, Annie's pet tortoise, wanders around the garden all day – she's 75 years old, and Annie tells me that she's only just approaching middle age!

I feel content and free here. I still have my worries, but this feels like home. It doesn't matter what's happening around me – when I come here, I feel peaceful. I like sitting in the lounge: it's comfortable and compact, and everything is lovely. There's a babbling brook across the road from us, and we often go for walks up the little lanes around us, or up onto Goss Moor with our spaniel, Jasper. We've got beautiful woodlands around us, with wonderful birds, amazing flowers and shrubs that are all different colours. The air is clean and fresh and I don't want to be anywhere else. It's the kind of place I dreamed of living in when I was a child.

22.

STILL BURNING

Although the purpose of this book is to tell my story, I am just the tip of a very large iceberg. The Child Migrants Trust estimates that more than 130,000 children were deported as part of the post-war migration programme, to places including Rhodesia (now called Zimbabwe), Canada, New Zealand, and Australia, where at least 8,000 were sent. This is the reason why I wanted to tell my story. It's a personal milestone for me, but it's also a record that I hope other people will read and say, "Did this really happen?" Although my story may be different from everyone else's, my experiences as a migrant are representative of thousands of others.

Margaret Humphreys blew the lid off the national scandal of child migration in the early 1990s when her book *Empty Cradles* was published, but it wasn't until 2010 that the British government did something more substantial in recognition of what had happened. In February of that year, the prime minister Gordon Brown apologised for the UK government's role in sending all of us children abroad. He described the programme as "misguided" – which I think is rather too soft a word for it – before he continued:

> *"To all those former child migrants and their families [...] I say today we are truly sorry. They were let down. We are sorry they were allowed to be sent away at the time when they were most vulnerable. We are sorry that instead of caring for them, this country turned its back. We are sorry that the voices of these children were not always heard, their cries for help not always heeded. And we are sorry that it has taken so long for this important day to come and for the full and unconditional apology that is justly deserved.*

He said that they had been cruelly lied to and "robbed" of their childhoods, and described the scheme as a shameful "deportation of the innocents". This all struck a chord with me, and it felt like a big thing. The issue of child migration is still buried, and people find it difficult to relate to what people like me have been through. When Gordon

Brown apologised, it felt like we were finally getting some recognition – people could understand a bit better what had happened, who was responsible, and how it had affected our whole lives. The issue was all over the press, people started talking to me about it more, and I was invited to do media appearances as well. But then the silence returned.

I think the next step should have been compensation and redress for everybody involved, but it hasn't happened. Then I heard from Kevin in Australia that a firm of lawyers was seeking compensation on behalf of more than a hundred child migrants. He said that he had heard about a law firm called Hugh James, who litigate in big cases like this, and gave me the details. When I went onto their website, I saw a video of one of the partners, Sam Parker, talking about migrants taking action. I contacted him, explaining what had happened to me, and we had a chat. Then he sent me an email with the details of his partner Alan Collins, who was leading the case in the UK, and asked if would I like to meet him.

Alan came and visited me, as well as a friend of mine called Ken, another child migrant. I liked Alan straight away. He wasn't playing power games – he was informally dressed, and seemed relaxed and honest and calm. He told me about what he'd been doing so far and what he wanted to happen next – he feels that the British government should pay compensation to all the child migrants who are still alive. He told me that he feels it is a morally compelling case, but the problem is that if the British government contests it, there could be years of legal wrangling, and in the meantime, people who were child migrants are dying. Jesus, I might even die before this thing gets sorted out! But it seems clear that the government doesn't want to deal with this issue – if you're looking at it cynically, maybe they're just waiting for all of us to die so that they don't have to pay compensation.

I asked Alan how much the case would cost me, and he told me it would cost me nothing at all, because he would charge the government. He then interviewed Ken, before heading off. I came away feeling quite stunned by it all – mainly by having free access to legal services.

It seems to me that the words spoken by Gordon Brown in his apology were completely hollow – unless they are backed up by a formal process of redress, they are meaningless. Personally, I don't believe that we will ever receive full compensation from the government. We've had an apology, but I don't think there will be anything else. In the summer of 2018 there was talk that Theresa May was going to get involved, but it didn't happen. A Labour MP called Lisa Nandy has been doing a lot of work on the issue of child migrants, and in August 2018 Alan Collins and I were invited onto the Victoria Derbyshire show on the BBC. It was live television, but I didn't have to go to London or Manchester for it – I went to Radio Cornwall in Truro, where they put me on a video feed to the main studio. That same day, I was on two other shows: Lawrence Reed interviewed me on Radio Cornwall and I also spoke on BBC Radio 5 Live. I told them about my experiences and slammed the council, who had apparently claimed that they'd apologised to me. Well, they hadn't. The bloke who came round to see me didn't apologise, and I haven't ever had a letter from them. There's no sincerity, and they've never tried to make up for what they did to me. All they've done is put a poxy article on their website, but I only found that quite recently because someone mentioned it to me.

There are lots of people who were involved in what happened to me: the Social Services Department at Cornwall Council, the contemptible Fairbridge Society, and the Tasmanian authorities, but for all the blame heaped on Fairbridge and the council, the truth is that it was the Home Secretary, which in autumn 1970 was Reginald Maudling, who signed off the papers that put me on that plane at Heathrow.

Why didn't the authorities put us in touch with my auntie and uncle, who were only four miles away from us when we were at the home in Newquay? It stinks, and

I wouldn't be surprised if backhanders were involved. For one thing, the policy was apparently not to split families, but if that was true, why did they only put two of us three in a home, and only send two of us to Australia? Why not Bruce? And why us two, out of thousands of kids? We were essentially used as little slaves in Tasmania – was there money involved, and did it go through Fairbridge? There must have been some incentive beyond the absurd idea that going to Australia would be "good for us", and I refuse to believe that there was no financial element.

A report that I read recently said that children from the Fairbridge homes "weren't integrating" into wider society in Australia – and that, for me, is clear proof that something was going badly wrong. Apparently, Fairbridge helped to supply "white stock" to Australia. That says it all, really – it makes us sound like cattle that had been organised by race. There's no way I could've known that at the time. But there was a regime – and the less you followed it, the more you were punished. What went on, and what people didn't see behind the scenes, is mind-boggling.

I've spent years digging for information and hitting brick walls. In 2000 the Freedom of Information Act came in, but I still hit brick walls, because I only got what the authorities thought I was entitled to see, which wasn't the whole truth. I didn't like the file that the Tasmanian authorities had sent me back in 2006, but at least I had it – I had been asking Fairbridge to show me my file since the late 1970s. I have a copy of a letter that a kind lady called Sheila Ryan from the Youth Support Unit in Launceston, Tasmania, wrote to the Fairbridge Society in 1981:

> *"I believe it is imperative for Rex's emotional and psychological stability (and also his right) to be able to make contact with any members of his immediate family or close relatives as soon as possible. In Tasmania the Fairbridge Society has closed its doors and has refused to assist Rex in his search. His only hope of assistance now is your society in London, as we have exhausted every other avenue here."*

One of the replies that I received in 1981 to my own letters to Fairbridge was an absolute disgrace. The letter, written by the "director" – no name is given – basically discouraged me from returning to England. His first point was that unemployment in Britain was high at the time, and that I would be financially better off staying in Tasmania. His second point was as follows:

"I assume that you are now [an] Australian citizen. In that case, it is very unlikely that the British Government would give you a permit to enter Britain: Australians coming to Britain these days are normally only given temporary entry visas."

The organisation that sent me to Australia in the first place was now telling me that I probably had no right to return the country of my birth: I couldn't believe what I was reading, and their unwillingness to offer any help or support persisted for a further three decades. They sent a partial version of my file in 1993, but it was 37 years, longer than my dad's lifetime, before I received a complete copy of my file from them. I am not just angry with them for what they did in the first place; I am also angry about the decades of obstruction and cover-up. Fairbridge is now run by the Prince's Trust. I recently telephoned them to ask for a further copy of my file, as I had misplaced my original, and they told me that I had to write a letter to the Prince's Trust to get their permission to access my files. That's crap – they knew my name and who I was, so why couldn't they give it to me? This is the sort of thing that happens every time I want information. It's obvious that they don't really give a monkey's about me, but why didn't they just do it as a gesture to show that they care? The truth is that they don't.

When I did eventually receive the copy of my file, I went through the whole thing. It is always upsetting and bewildering to reread my case from the start. There are many letters from me in this file, asking for more information, help, and access to my file. One of them, from 1983, is particularly angry, but it asks the questions that I still haven't had satisfactory answers to.

Dear Sir,

I have had the opportunity of writing to you and your organisation on numerous occasions, requesting your assistance in the locating of my "family", who it seems have no idea whatsoever as to what happened to me so many years ago.

It seems that you and your organisation have failed most miserably and negligently in your administrative duties.

Letters received from various relatives over the past twelve months, have invariably asked the same basic questions: "What are you doing all the way over there?" and "How come we were not informed?"

It seems to me, without a doubt, that your organisation is incompetent in the light of not carrying out administrative duties to the fullest. Was it so hard for you to find someone to ask about me?

A letter received by me, from one of my relatives in England, reeks of untruth. Your organisation has in a fashion blatantly lied to them. If you had taken the opportunity to read the files on me, you would without a shadow of doubt have found it absolutely impossible for me to come to Tasmania with either one of my parents. [...]

The point I wish to emphasise is that you let me at the tender age of 11 make such a vast decision.

So consequently you shipped me off to some faraway place, and now you are able to sit back and wait for some more bait.

You only seem to ship people one way. I have asked for your organisation's help in trying to return to my homeland.

I am still a British subject, regardless of what you think or say. Surely, if you can send a person one way, then you can and should retrieve them.

I have never liked what was done to me, and will never forgive your organisation for your incompetence.

I would gratefully appreciate a reply, on the understanding that my questions are answered and that justice will be done to correct a wrong.

Yours sincerely,
Rex Wade

Who was ultimately to blame for what happened to me? Cornwall County Council organised it in the first place, Fairbridge made it happen, the Home Office signed the necessary paperwork and the Tasmanian authorities were fully complicit: in my eyes, they are all equally responsible. The fact is that even now, when I want a piece of information, I am made to jump over another barrier. Here I am, almost 40 years after I started trying to find out what happened to me, and I'm still not getting clear answers. What have they got to hide? The whole thing stinks of an establishment cover-up: people not wanting to lose their reputations over a bunch of scruffy kids in care who were sent to Australia. It's the same with the council. One of the councillors came round to see me and said that they'd already apologised.

"If you try to sue us, we'll tie it up for years."

It was a warning: don't even bother. He gave me his card and I phoned him a few weeks later, but no one in his department had heard of him. Who the hell had come to see me? The council have also been uncooperative – my lawyer has asked for documents from them, and they haven't provided a thing.

In Australia, my brother Kevin received a letter from the government there, inviting him to attend at ceremony in October 2018 at which the Australian Prime Minister Scott Morrison was to give an official apology to all those children who had endured sexual abuse in care. My brother turned down the invitation because he was not sexually abused. It's difficult to unpack the different forms of abuse: physical, mental, and sexual abuse all have their origins in powerlessness. The problem was that when we arrived there, we were put in a position where people were not looking after our welfare.

Every state in Australia has now granted compensation settlements for all child migrants, and yet the British government has not. I hope that the British government will one day follow the Australian lead, but I'm not sure that it will.

What happened to my mother had remained a mystery ever since I first found out I was adopted. Not knowing her has been the biggest sadness of my life. But recently new information has come to light – though it only served to increase the agony of my never meeting her.

I discovered that my mother, Marina Violet Wade, outlived my father by over 40 years. In fact, she was still alive when Annie and I got married. The thought that she could have come to our wedding, that we could have been reunited on what was already the happiest day of my life, is possibly the hardest thing of all to take.

My mother died of cancer in Bristol on 13 August 2008. If only the authorities had released the information I spent so much of my adult life requesting, I could have met her. I could have got to know the woman who gave life to me. There would have been time for me to hear the story of our family, which has remained shrouded in mystery for so long.

But this did not happen. By ignoring my pleas, denying me the one thing I was desperate to know, the authorities deprived me of the opportunity to make peace with my mother, to meet her again in person, to talk to her, to understand her. And when I finally found out what had happened to her, it was 10 years too late.

I hope to visit her grave one day. In 2016, after months of research with my cousin Mike, I found out where my father is buried − and going to see his grave near Bodmin has helped me to come to terms with the realities of my childhood and upbringing. But the fact that I spent so long unaware of the fact that my mother was still alive is a sadness that will never leave me.

But as I have so often found in my life, even in the darkest times there is always hope. What I do know is that my mother had another daughter after she remarried. Her daughter, my half-sister, was born in 1964 in Plymouth, and I hope that one day I will be able to meet her. I didn't reach my mother in time, but I hope at least to find my half-sister. I hope she can tell me what my mother was like.

My biggest regret is not knowing my son, Josh, who has grown up in Tasmania without me, and who will now be in his late thirties. To Josh I simply want to say that I'm sorry, and I hope that if you ever read this book it might help you understand some of the bad things I've done in my life, even if it does not excuse them.

I have destroyed my body with my lifestyle: I was an alcoholic for 30 years and have smoked since I was 10. I now vape rather than smoke, and barely drink, but the damage has been well and truly done. I have neglected myself, and for much of my life, I deliberately set out to harm myself because I wanted to erase who I was.

I have to take an incredible amount of medication every day. I have survived suicide attempts, two heart attacks, nervous breakdowns, clinical depression, osteoarthritis, liver disease, a total knee replacement and while writing this book, I have had half of my right lung removed because of a malignant tumour. All this feels like a real shame, because I have finally managed to get to a place where I am completely happy, with a woman who has been patient and loving and kind and wonderful, but I don't know how much time I have left to enjoy it. So I treat every day as special, and make the most of it.

I have never felt comfortable in my own skin and I still

sometimes struggle with it, but I am increasingly able to accept myself for who I am. The rage has died down; there is still a deep-rooted anger deep inside me, but most of the time I am calm and measured and I have learned to let my softer side come out. I am not ashamed of that – I've realised that it's good to be kind and gentle and compassionate as often as possible. I only tried it after a lifetime of anger and fighting and punching walls, but it feels good.

These feelings and ways of behaving have always been there, but I think that earlier in my life they were hidden by my need to conform to some idea of what it means to be a man. I sometimes have a good cry, and sometimes it really helps. Every morning, I wake up next to Annie, make myself a cup of tea, and go for a potter outside with Jasper. I look at the flowers and look up at the sky and listen to the sound of the birds and the spring water coming down from the hill. I breathe in as much fresh air as my one-and-a-half lungs will allow, because to me, it smells like uncontained freedom and joy. And at that moment, I love life and I want as much of it as possible. I want to breathe in as much of it as I can and to have as much happiness and laughter and joy as possible, before I take a well-deserved rest for the final time.

Acknowledgements

I'd like to thank Annie, the most important person in my life, who has been an incredible companion, a great listener, and a wonderful and fun person to spend my life with. I am so glad I met you, Annie – without you, I could never have even contemplated writing this book.

I also want to thank Annie's very supportive children, Eebie, Janie and Cathy, who accepted me into their wonderful family and have been kind to me even when I've been short-tempered with them.

I've had very different relationships with my brothers Kevin and Bruce, but they mean a lot to me and I'm glad to be able to speak to them both now.

Thank you to the Child Migrants Trust for their help, and for the incredible service they provide to all the other child migrants out there.

Thanks too to my cousins Mike and Rosie and to my good friend Benny, who never judged and who always accepted and supported me.

Thanks to Kevin Telfer, who has helped me tell my story.

Thank you to Ajda Vucicevic at Mirror Books who commissioned this book, believed in my story and has always been caring throughout the process. And a special thank you to George Robarts, for his help with this book. George, I am particularly grateful for your vision, editorial input and enthusiasm for making this book the best it can be.

Also by Mirror Books

1963 - A Slice of Bread and Jam
Tommy Rhattigan

Tommy lives at the heart of a large Irish family in derelict Hulme in Manchester, ruled by an abusive, alcoholic father and a negligent mother. Alongside his siblings he begs (or steals) a few pennies to bring home to avoid a beating, while looking for a little adventure of his own along the way.

His foul-mouthed and chaotic family may be deeply flawed, but amongst the violence, grinding poverty and distinct lack of hygiene and morality lies a strong sense of loyalty and, above all, survival.

During this single year – before his family implodes and his world changes for ever – Tommy almost falls foul of the welfare officers, nuns, police – and Myra Hindley and Ian Brady.

An adventurous, fun, dark and moving true story of the only life young Tommy knew.

m
B

Also by Mirror Books

Boy Number 26
Tommy Rhattigan

**From the Sunday Times Bestselling author of
1963: A Slice of Bread and Jam**

Little Tommy Rhattigan was taken into care in 1964 aged just 8, where he entered a closed off world of institutionalised sexual abuse.

Moved from a care home in Manchester to a reform school in Liverpool, the state was supposed to pick up the duty of care that his parents had failed to give. But instead, young Tommy was separated from his brother, and thrown to the wolves.

Tommy Rhattigan takes us back to his own childhood of pranks, cruelty and laughter, grown from a need to survive his daily torment and to stick two fingers up to the system that was failing him so spectacularly.

m
B

Also by Mirror Books

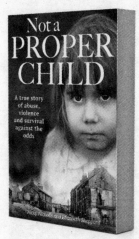

Not A Proper Child
Nicky Nicholls and Elizabeth Sheppard

Left as a newborn in a box outside Stoke City Football ground, Nicky's grandparents took her into their home, but instead of finding refuge - she was subjected to sexual abuse. In 1951, at the age of six, her estranged mother 'rescued' her. But Nicky's hopes of a safe and loving home were soon dashed, and her world became darker still...

As a result of her broken young life, Nicky spent years as a homeless alcoholic, ending up in prison, where she encountered Moors Murderer Myra Hindley and glimpsed pure evil.

Nicky's compelling life story captures her rare spirit of survival against the odds, and charts her rise from the horror of a deeply damaging childhood to a positive, creative and independent life.

mB

Also by Mirror Books

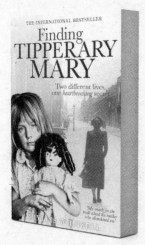

THE INTERNATIONAL BESTSELLER

Finding Tipperary Mary
Phyllis Whitsell

The astonishing real story of a daughter's search for her own past
and the desperate mother who gave her up for adoption.

Phyllis Whitsell began looking for her birth mother as a young woman and although it was many years before she finally met her, their lives had crossed on the journey without their knowledge.
When they both eventually sat together in the same room,
the circumstances were extraordinary, moving and
ultimately life-changing.

This is a daughter's personal account of the remarkable
relationship that grew from abandonment into love,
understanding and selfless care.

mB